I0135175

Daddy's Girl

A Memoir in Poetry
Safrianna Lughna

Daddy's Girl
Copyright © 2024 by Safrianna Lughna, also under the aliases A_Jade_Moon
and A.J. Eastwood.
All rights reserved.

No portion of this book may be reproduced in any form without written
permission from the publisher or author, except as permitted by U.S. copyright
law.

Lughna, Safrianna
First edition
ISBN: 979-8-9907819-1-7

Cover designed by S. Lughna on CanvaPro.
Interior layout by S. Lughna with Atticus.
Visual elements designed in CanvaPro by S. Lughna and Justin Ebersole.
Manuscript edited by the Living LUNA Publishing Team, S. Lughna and J.
Ebersole.

To contact the author, send an email to Author@Safrianna.com

MADE IN THE USA

Works By Safrianna Lughna

Poetry
A Woman's Work
Daddy's Girl

Fiction
Bumble Bees & White Balloons

For the most up to date book listings, go to:
Safrianna.com/author

Content Warning

Do not read past this if you do not want spoilers of poetry book content, though no details are given. However, **this book contains potentially triggering material!**

Some readers may find content in this poetry book highly personal and difficult. This manuscript deals with sensitive content including: domestic violence, sexual abuse and assault, self-harm, religious trauma (specifically Christian), child abuse, neglect, incest, misogyny/sexism, miscarriage, self-esteem and body-based issues, LGBTQIA+ related topics, eating disorders, and other potentially triggering topics. This book is not intended to be read by those who find such content offensive or re-traumatizing.

Please use appropriate coping skills and tools if you find yourself overwhelmed by any content herein and discontinue reading.

Contents

Preface

Why It Was Time to Share *Daddy's Girl*

The curse of generational trauma has pervaded our planet for so long that it seems hardly any of us can imagine a better way. Our health and closeness are in crisis from bloodlines continually passing down unhealthy behaviors and systems. There is enough pain from natural disasters, illness, and death. We don't need to create more suffering for one another. Yet we do.

One of the most common wounds I've witnessed in my years as a teacher, therapist, and guide are familial wounds—created in relationships with our parents or childhood caregivers.

Almost everyone I've held space for shared a story of their elders harming them in some way:

— emotional neglect, not making space for children's feelings

— emotional abuse, such as the all too common, "Stop crying or I'll give you something to cry about"

— no room for self-expression, lack of autonomy given, pushing children to do what they don't want to

— birth time traumas and/or adoption and separation traumas

— sexual trauma, or stories of not being believed or protected from exploitation

— being forced into caregiving and reversed parent-child roles early and without consent or understanding

— neglect in all forms, poverty, and lack of access to basic survival needs

I could re-tell hundreds of stories of pain and suffering caused by humans being inconsiderate of their impact on others. By avoiding looking at their unprocessed pain, it pours out in their behaviors—how they treat their loved ones and community; how they handle triggers, grief, shame, disappointment, and fear.

I've seen and heard so much trauma from my clients and students that I could fill volumes on it. However, *Daddy's Girl* isn't a collection of case studies. It's a raw, honest telling of my perspective of my relationship with my father and the complex grief I experienced in his passing. Through that, I found myself over time—unpacked my patterns of over-giving of myself and reclaimed my voice. *Daddy's Girl* is my story, my snapshot of the intersections of our lives, and the circumstances that forged me in shimmering steel.

It's important to me to acknowledge that as I write, I am always writing from my perspective. I can't account for other's thoughts and feelings, and anywhere I express things about others or a situation, it is my view. I have dealt with dissociation through much of my life, and bits and pieces of my memories have come and gone with various traumas, moments of peace, and awareness.

In all of my writing, I keep any people still living intentionally vague. I see people who have passed as humans with their own complex, often messy lives. For both living and dead, I forgive and release all contracts and mutual burdens held between us. That includes my late father, who as you'll uncover, I had a very challenging relationship with.

I wrote 47 of my 79 poems in *Daddy's Girl* during the period of time when my father was rapidly declining and continued drafting until months after his death. I began writing sometime around when I helped with his will and created in a flurry after my final hospital visit with him. After my father passed, I took my last trip back to New

York to desperately attempt to salvage his estate while my other parents made demands. My sister and I were still in shock and recovering from so much damn trauma. Instead of taking a collective breather and time to mourn, I endured the klaxon call of compulsory codependent behaviors and generational stories constantly blaring in my ears. It was *not* a good time.

While I'm okay with it all now, I was also deeply impacted by it, too. This project helped me process, honor, and release these wounds—for myself and others.

Like many of our fathers—unfortunately tangled up in patriarchal bullshit—my father struggled with sexism, racism, biphobia, transphobia, substance abuse, and treated various people in his life in unsupportive ways. He also slowly killed himself at work, and threw his all into trying to be the provider in a financial sense, though he never seemed to have any money. He was complicated, and I'll never know his whole story.

But, it's time to speak my story, and now.

Too many of us are wounded children grown into brokenhearted, lost adults. We wander, seeking connection, understanding, and love. If we're brave, we can find it as we heal from the painful separateness we felt when we were younger.

We've survived collective traumas, many of which we still remember and even more we don't.

If we had better relationships with our fathers... If our fathers had better relationships with their fathers and mothers... If the generational chain was not tarnished from centuries of families bleeding rust...

Imagine life then.

These sorts of pains—the vulnerable, most private pains of childhood—can only be resolved through communication, compassion, and boundaries.

Unfortunately, boundaries are impossible to set when we are children if we are around unhealthy adults. Children truly have no say in what they endure, save to try and run away or tell another adult. They don't have a car or necessarily know how to look up and call for services. They might not even have access to outward communication at all. But as adults, there are more possibilities.

As adults, we may be *stuck* in many of the same patterns perpetuated in our childhoods, and fresh cycles created in complex, often codependent adult relationships. We may be terrified to draw boundaries, to say no, or to remove ourselves from situations that hurt because that's what we're used to. We often reenact childhood dynamics trying to prove we can "fix" the pain.

But that's not how it works.

So long as we stay silent, the same swirls of shame and fear will haunt us.

And I shall stay silent and stuck no more.

I stand with survivors of generational trauma in solidarity, raising a rallying cry for better for us all. It will take communication, compassion, curiosity, and presence to create better, but I believe we can do it.

I believe we can heal ourselves and, thus, the world.

Thank you for picking up this book and for going on my journey of grief with me. May this collection of poems bring you closer to yourself and deepen your care for each other.

All My Love,

Safrianna Lughna, LCPC, MS
The Queer-Spirit Guide
Author, Speaker, CEO

Acknowledgments

Thank you to my pre-alpha, mid-despair phase readers, Ikenna and Ariel. Both of you read the initial drafts of *Daddy's Girl* written during unyielding waves of grief, anger, and confusion. Without your support during the messy "*Doing it live*" times, I don't know how I would have survived. I barely got through the turmoil of my father's estate falling to shambles and failed to mourn in the moment. Thank you for supporting me in expressing myself through poems. I appreciate you both with all my heart, and thank you for doing what you could to support me.

Thank you to Robin Kinzer of *Robin's Nest*, my dear merfriend, poet and editor. Who knew eating vegan Chinese food when we first met would lead to such a magical series of events? We inspired an even greater love and focus on poetry in each other. I owe so many of our conversations and connections through swapping poems to the birth of this body of work. Thank you for helping me reunite with the Poet and Unicorn energy within me, and for being my first professional developmental editor.

Thank you to my incredible alpha reader and co-editor, Justin Ebersole. You are my partner in the war against manuscript software glitches and typos. Between us putting our heads together to polish the third draft and every moment spent finessing the final product, I enjoy your companionship on my writing projects. This one felt extra special in what it brought up for each of us during the final read-throughs. Thank you for always supporting me to be my best.

A special shout-out to each of my incredible beta readers who got to see the semi-final poems and give last-minute feedback. I hope you enjoy the visual additions in the print copy. Thank you for the support, cheerleading, and, of course, for catching some of those errors that zip by like comets after I've read the same words twelve times in a week already. I am grateful to each of you!

—Rachel Warmath, Author of *Alive in the Fire*
—Dawn Sullivan, Author of *The Aurora Keys*
—Carrie Dennison, Owner of Self-Care with Carrie
—Dorey M. Kern, Magical Mentor
—Sol Obsidian, Embodied Manifestation Guide
—Starling Hathcock

Each of you affirmed the importance and power of my story. Thank you for sharing resonance and love with me.

Dedication

I dedicate this poetry collection to all my fellow humans with #daddyissues.

To the brave souls overcoming generational trauma—I see you, and I believe you.

DADDY'S GIRL

Daddy's Girl

A badge I wore, proud
to be his daughter 'til he
refused to believe.

CRACKED
FOUNDATIONS

This is My Story

[[I look back, or I guess it's more fitting to say I
                    Float Back—
Drifting as I've often done, wraithlike,
in my attempts to put all the pieces together.

This time is different. This time, I am in control.
This time, I collect the fragments with confidence.

It's soothing, settling, to realize I've mastered the
scattered puzzle before me on the table—
made it whole.

I did that. I put myself back together. I twisted my brain
around the mystery of me until I realized I was never lost—
only entombed in the expectations of my Elders,
suffocating beneath their burdens and beliefs.

So, I'll build a foundation—speak my story—because
this is the end, beginning.]]

Life Lessons

My Dad taught me:

• Money, all green and glimmer, is more important
than anything, especially when I have none.

• Always put others first, even if it pushes me over
an invisible ledge, plummets me into unhealth and
agony. (Hide the mottled circles beneath my weary eyes.
Carry on.)

• Promises are paths to getting what I desire—but others
never keep them. That would mean respecting
boundaries—and boundaries aren't real, just a flash, a
twinkle, an inkling.

• Queer identities are phantoms; I might think they're
there, but if I look close enough, I'll see the fallacy.
There are two genders tied to biological sex markers—
I'm either gay or straight as no other orientation exists.

• My word as a female is not law: it is lies.
I "take after" my mother; a woman no better than Lilith.

First wife. She-demon. Temptress.

• A woman's body is not her own, aside from working it;
it belongs in the male gaze. Suck in that gut and ignore
its feelings at the same time. This is a mere rental, and
I must pay preciously.

• Be secretive. Be quiet. Fume in the dark, like pale
blue smoke collecting in corners where light cannot reach,
ready to dissipate if anyone else blows through.

• It's not worth trying to be seen as whole. Forever,
I will exist in a fractured mirror: her father's eyes reflected,
his nose, his teeth, the muddy sweep of his cowlick, but the
image is no more than a sad girl longing for a little time.

Blank Pages

I wish I had more memories of my father
doting on me. Of him holding my hand.
Him chuckling at his own Dad Jokes.

Instead, I have blank pages. Occasionally,
there are splatters of ink that make vague
shapes of memories: him, asleep on the couch;
him, coveting a Honda Civic like some elusive treasure;
him, acting like he was 20 when really he was 40,
so hip in his baggy pants and jangling wallet chain,
fresh from Hot Topic.

Sometimes, there are splashes of color: us
watching a robot anime; him renting a Game Shark
so I could beat Final Fantasy X—my lifeline—
before I left for school in the fall; him taking
me to work with him when I was 4, forgetting me
as he disappeared through the Developmental Center
doors where the boy with empty eye sockets offered me
more connection, authenticity, truth.

Often, I am left making up stories, or at least
trying to fill in the empty spots.

On good days, I color in the white space with
vibrant love, splitting laughter.

I scribble out the evil stepmother and pretend
she never tore our family picture apart with her
sharp words like scattered shards of glass. Pretend
I didn't grow up witnessing her shredded wrists.
Pretend there aren't empty lines for years and years,
no distance between my father and I.

When I think too hard about all those barren
books, chapters that will never be written or
torn out before we could make something
of them, I feel bitter. I wanted better for us.

Empty-handed, I turn towards myself, inward,
finding the fountain pen with
which to write my own story.

Pasta and Sauce

In my childhood, poverty looked like:
— growling stomach eating itself for brunch followed by
blue boxes of rigatoni, raging red jars of sauce every
weeknight, La Choy chow mein (in the double stacked cans)
as a "treat." Once in a while greasy boxes of pizza—even
better for the rare breakfast the following morning
— being left to raise my siblings and cousins because
childcare was out of reach
— going window shopping at Wegmans, wondering why I
couldn't get the toys or books I wanted, why my friend's
houses looked so different, so full of *possibility*
— outgrown clothing bisecting my belly into segments, my
body insectoid, straining against cloth constraints, distorted
forever
— hiding in the dressing room at the Limited Too on a
field trip crying because none of the clothes fit—this being
my only chance to try on fancy, frilly dresses or chic silver
jumpsuits before jaunting down a runway
— despair, damnation, brushing abuse under dirty rugs

In the Spacelab

My sister and I picked up on our father's
love of sci-fi early. Played pretend often on the
dilapidated treadmill in Great Grandmother's
basement. With blankets draped over the
metal arms and stickers between our eyes, we
became Alien captains of The Heart Starship,
a vessel where we could fly beyond all that
kept us small.

Our imaginations could take us anywhere,
far away from the threats of Hell,
another poverty pasta night, the tense
evenings when Mom and Dad fought. We imagined
we could glide away from early-onset sexual abuse,
rocket past our confusing childhoods, coast into
a future where we'd be in charge of our trajectory—
whether the ship slips the stream and crashes,
or we soar free into the limitless sky—a
destination determined by our own hands.

The Kindhearted Stranger

Around the time I started fearing Hell, I also met a man in my head: A Protector.

Like moth to moon, beneath heaps of blankets, gasping between sobs, I submerged into dread convinced any moment the lightning strike of a spiteful Biblical God would find me unworthy of another breath. By 4-years-old, I knew I must go inside, find that holy aspect, the benevolent God within.

The scenario in my nighttime musings was routine. Life was a miserable marathon, confusing, unyielding, spiraling towards hopelessness in dark places where I was left alone. So, I'd run away from home in my head to gather glimpses of redemption like rotting treasures.

I found my way to a bright beacon—my own Daddy Warbucks—a benign benefactor who without expectation other than me being myself, provided me a sanctuary where I could live freely, create, express, and above all, be safe.

He was clear like words in relief blooming on a page in the darkness: tall, dark, and handsome, a series of qualities that by the time I could speak, I believed was an ideal of masculinity to be desired. Wearing a black suit and tie, he stood on the marble staircase of his mansion, arms outspread, waiting for me to arrive.

In my vision, my heart blooms—I can feel the warmth, support, permission from him. I glide into his arms, he plucks me up, takes me inside to find the luxuries awaiting me—endless art supplies, a stunning space of my own where I can read or play alone, a wardrobe full of clothes I adore and fit, a common room where I can enjoy community, eat wholesome meals surrounded by loving people who do not condemn me to damnation.

No longer a stranger, my Inner Father has nothing but love for me—receives the same in return: he is my proper picture of the sacred masculine, structure, tenderness, safety I'd never know again until my thirties.

One day, he vanished into the fog of obscurity along with those childhood dreams of solace—but I know he lives on, a seed that's grown into a brilliant beam of light blooming in my chest, bursting into a thousand glittering fireflies, sunsets, summer heat storms, mirth reflected in my man's eyes as we sway on the porch to my heart song.

Papa and the Cows

Sometimes, I wonder if it was easier for my father
to condemn me because I was constantly called by
mother's name—cognitive dissonance splaying her face
over mine every time we spoke. Did that syllable distort his
perceptions until he believed I was more like her than him?

You see, Papa, my maternal grandfather, suffered a
double-brain aneurysm before my sister was born. In the
process, his retention of things, especially names, went up
in a flash like lint used for tinder—dissipated in a blink.

Papa was the man of my mother's heart—the ideal depiction
of healthy, supportive masculinity. Despite her complicated
relationship with her mother, I spent many of my early years
with her parents—cuddled up with Papa, watching shows
or sitting in the same space silently with Grandma while we
parallel-processed with creativity.

Predating any of my conscious memories, Papa picked me
up often, set me in his lap, and let me collect Junior Mint

candies from his breast pocket. There are buried polaroids of us—me covered in cake on my 1st birthday, Papa smiling, cognizant of who I was—his daughter's daughter—his granddaughter.

After his medical episodes, who I was vanished. Instead of being plucked up, I curled up with him in his home-hospital bed, playing with the controls to get comfy. We'd watch TV—whatever was on cable in the early 1990s. Or, on even better days when the weather was nice, we'd sit on the porch built onto the side of Grandma and Papa's doublewide trailer, parked on an acre of land overlooking verdant pastures and cornfields.

Between the brain bleeds and escalating multiple sclerosis, Papa's memory was about as effective as a wire fence trying to contain a flood. He remembered his wife's name—Marie—and my mother's—not specifically for her, but for anyone who vaguely looked like her. And so, I was never myself with him but a miniature mother, always called by her name. I didn't mind. He couldn't even remember he told the same stories whenever we were together.

Gazing out at the farm hill in the distance, skyline punctuated only by powerlines, Papa would chuckle, orienting his wheelchair towards the rolling green grasses. He'd clear his throat and say—"Did I ever tell you about the cows?" Yes, he had, but I lived for these moments of mirth.

His cheeks were like glossy red apples as he'd laugh, tears pricking his eyes as he'd amp up to tell the full story for the hundredth time. "I remember once, this big ol' bull was trying to get fresh with some of the heifers, right up on that hill! Well, that bull, he picked the wrong girl one day. He was getting up in her face, and she was having none of it. He wouldn't let up, and finally, she whipped around and kicked him right down the hill. That bull!!!" He'd gasp laughing, unable to move his hands much to gesticulate in the later days. "He went a'tumbling down that hill, rolling! Served him right getting fresh with a lady who didn't want it!"

Oh, if only the other men in my life would be so chivalrous as my paraplegic Papa. Skeletons in all the closets but his, save perhaps, for his flirtations with quite consenting women. It'd be a long time until I'd find a man as safe, wholesome, and sweet as Papa—a simple man who enjoyed watching the cows chew clover, cheered on women's rights, and loved his wife 'til death and beyond.

ripped

In the shifting shadows of blades and branches
on a pink and perfect sunlit summer evening,
I was ripped from the nest I'd built in the
Maple tree out back.

I revered that tree. A friend, my first love, and home.
Certainly, home.

Her limbs helped me climb each day to new sights,
Her rich brown trunk was my body outside me.
Her three-pointed leaves, ever so slightly translucent,
showcased her darkened veins as sunbeams shone through.
Her seeds, flinging themselves at the ground, fluttered like
cicada wings—teaching me I could fly in my own way, too.

Maple taught me of myself. Helped me find the secrets
hiding in the deepest places within my cavernous core,
silent corners where cobwebs might collect if not
for Her intervention.

She was a Mother Tree if ever in my life I have met one,

her boughs tender, rough bark caressing my skin.

I desperately desired my Father's approval, still
longing for him to see me, my sparkle, my sweetness, my
vibrant spirit. Looking back, I see Maple tried to show me
my magic. Show me what I was, really—why he could not
see.

I was like the faeries I witnessed dancing around the
tree—there, but gone in a glimmer if you look too close.
Perhaps Dad had gone wonder-blind, too jaded by
the world (and my mother) who had mistreated him so.

And I — I was a wonder to behold.

So when I stood in those shifting shadows, me, 8,
my then-still-silly sister, 4, and we were told to
pick a parent to live with, I was torn in three.

Choose my Mother who had birthed me,
my Father, who I longed so much to know me, or
maternal Maple, who had witnessed more of
my tears and troubles than any other living being.

Too wounded to choose, I thrust the task upon my sister in
the driveway, still sunlit, but no longer perfect.
I knew, either way, I'd have to part with Maple;
I could not bury myself with Her roots; climb to Her
tallest branches. Whether I chose "home" hundreds of
miles away or still dozens, the yard which housed

Her was to be relinquished, out of my reach.

Decades later, I still miss Her. Think of Her. Every tree
I witness with three-pointed leaves, seeds like cicada wings,
strong, tough trunks, and soothing souls, reminds me—
I want nothing more than to be
cradled in the nest of Her arms.

Toxic Triangles

Therapists often talk about triangulation—a tactic used to divide and conquer—get desired results through indirect communication, often behind other's backs. I had an early lesson on the dangers of this method—how not talking as a group can protect the egos of those holding tight to power—preserving their desires at all costs.

When Mom asked, "Do you want to live in New York with your Dad or move to Maryland with me?" breath flooded from my lungs. I froze. I could not compute, could not find the correct answer in the sprawl of stories that spread out before me. I fled to ask my sister: "Do you want to live with Mom or Dad?"

My sister thought about it, answered: "Mom." Not because that's what she wanted, but because she thinks I want that outcome. I don't know what I want. I'm 8. She's 4. We come to the agreement like two spaceships sending quantum signals galaxies apart—unaware of the vast darkness we'll cross to get to our eventual destinations.

Nonetheless, a decision is made. A decision that will strip us down to only the innocence held in reserve by our soul sparks.

Dad doesn't protest in front of us. Doesn't talk about his side for years. Later uses the whole situation to villainize Mom—how she just wanted more money in the form of child support.

He doesn't address how he could have handled it differently, defended us, or how no adult should ask a 4 and 8-year-old to make massive life decisions without even providing them a bit of the big picture.

He doesn't even see how I am playing mediator between their adult dramas, again, always the hinge in their toxic triangle.

print-a-kid

Tried not to sniffle too loudly that you weren't home

instead, vowed to get you to notice me
by any means necessary

played with pastel lego blocks at grandma's table
hopeful to make something I could show you
(I usually built villages)

collected Hot Wheels of your favorite cars, but
wanted to have a *real* Bitchin' Camaro, just like yours,
drive it like you did in Need For Speed,
breaking free, singing, "window to the wall"

blasted Aerosmith, AC/DC, Sex Pistols
anthems of rebellious youth though I was merely
conforming to your favorites, (except Rush.
I never got around to Rush, so there's my rebellion)

rubbed the rust off your rickety van, power tool in hand,
goggles on, in an outfit matching yours, black band t-shirt,
baggy jeans, big glasses: your mini-me—Did I complete you?

meanwhile, you snapped pictures, the kind you
drop off at drug stores, then wait for

that's what I was doing

Developing: trying to form myself after your image,
desperate for you to see

Roller Coasters & Water Slides

0.

Two things brought you and I together in our early days:
1) water slides
2) roller coasters

1) A smooth slipping slide,
cascading, circulating, the ebb, the flow,
the swelling swirl, water like a womb, vulnerable,
exposed in the flood, flying free,
rushing out toward the light,
a single colossal splash.

It's over.

2) The other loops you up and over,
down,

      around, twisting,

stomach flipping,

body racketing with force—jarring—
clattering teeth, hands gripping, wild in the air
without a care in all the fucked up world.

There were two incidents of note:
The kind that made me doubt my courage,
swallow lessons taught in metaphors like medicine.

I.

The first time I was 7.
Double tube, mini-you, big-me,
accelerating fast, facing the curve and mist,

weightless,

aloft
   on a soft cloud
made of rubber, buoyant.
Alive.

Bump. Big bounce. I am thrown
from my front-row seat to the
Ultimate Fun onto the inflexible
form of the water slide.

I careen through sapphire space—
solid, bendy child's bones
break my fall but don't shatter.

I spatter myself into the pool,
a skipping stone, sinking,
submerging,
breathing in chemicals,
lungs sting.

Stand somehow, shaking but straight.
Turn towards my savior, only to see
you, a bullet, shooting at me from the chute.

There's a crash. World topples into chlorine-blue blocks.
You have trampoline leapt using my skeleton as a net
and I'm drowning.

No more water slides, but a future full of being
bowled over by your opinions.

II.

The second joy gone-wrong, I was 11.
It was Spring vacation; I remember
only because I was embarrassed every day
of 6th grade I rode the elevator.

My desire to be a brave girl, impress you,
try something new, made me the
Crippled Girl because

suddenly

I smashed my spine against the seat of the
rickety wooden roller coaster. My back
gave out like a tree trunk in a woodchipper.

The injury was invisible—another hidden pain that
couldn't simply be scanned on a screen,
a prescription written for my woes.
Instead of being supported, I paid for
speaking up for all within me that needed attention.

I'd not walk upright for weeks,
collapsing inward into a crushed core;
feeling fractured, feelings ignored.

In the future, I'd only ride the coasters that
shone with the certainty of smooth metal frames,
no walls built to keep the inner workings, or me,

out of view.

Coda

I learned to engage with you only under specific
circumstances. Speak solely about what you deemed
appropriate. "Right." All else burrowed in my
vertebrae to hide.

Wishbone

Pull me at my arms, snap me in two,
Mom & Dad. See who can win the most
flattering fraction of my broken bones.

I'll Never Measure Up

By 1st grade, I learned I "couldn't spell" because
I was 99th percentile for everything except
ordering the letters in words—shamed for this
because I was "otherwise brilliant."

Well above the bell curve for height by 3rd grade,
I heard my destiny decreed over and over.
Dad announced, "You're going to be a basketball player."
I stopped growing at 5'5"—watched Space Jam tirelessly
but burst into tears whenever a ball came near me.

By 15, I knew I wasn't pretty enough, tall enough, smart
enough, needed to lose weight to survive, too *plump* to
succeed.

Fuck all the proportions our parents, doctors, schools
fixated on, like counts on a curve could determine
our worth or purpose—as if one percentile
on a number line could ever foretell the future.

Grandmas' Girl

Betty

By the time I was 5, I knew I looked "just like her," would be raised to be just like her. We rarely visited, but I heard stories. She was a hard-working woman who built her own home from the foundation up, though it was founded on generational trauma, the cracks scarring like splintered veins in seemingly unbreakable stone. She married her cousin young, didn't have to change her last name, had several sons and a daughter, all with scars sundering their sexual stories.

Knowing what I know now about post-traumatic stress disorder, my heart breaks to realize just how much perverse pain went silent through her bloodline, how much agony she carried in her womb, how much was passed on to be processed in the slow reclamation of my own voice—not just like her, but breaking the cycle of secrets so long left to suffocate our truth.

Marie

If there was an adult who really raised me, it was Marie—her frail hands like graceful spiders weaving webs where I could comfortably be my full self. She was the one who got me Goosebumps books, Polly Pockets, pastel Lego sets. She reintroduced me to my magic by buying me my first Harry Potter book. I saw myself in Hermione until book 7 where she lost herself—probably because I was losing myself in a marriage that mirrored my dynamics with my father. I digress.

Marie called me Freaky Friday in my teens, flashing crazy eyes at me as she wheeled around in her scooter at the nursing home to play innocent pranks on her peers—sprinkling confetti in their bedpans and having my problematic uncle stash a statue shark head in the parking lot garden. Sapped of strength as she was, her lungs blackened from decades of coping in pale clouds of smoke, she possessed the spirit of a sprite, ever seeking a last laugh.

When she passed, I was 16. My chest birthed a singularity as it caved in with the weight of realizing—I no longer had anyone living on Earth I knew loved me in all my queer, radical rebel Self without question.

Mini-Dad

Dad

‣ Brown hair, brown eyes, glasses, cowlick
‣ Age 41-43
‣ Baggy pants, wallet chain
‣ Love of anime, esp. hentai
‣ Works on cars, puts cool stripes on them (dreams of havin' a bitchin' camaro)

Me

‣ Brown hair (sometimes neon), brown eyes, rarely glasses, cowlick
‣ Age 13-15
‣ Baggy pants, cosmetic chain
‣ Love of anime, esp. Magical girls
‣ Works on cars, posing in photos to look cool for Dad while grinding rust off the side of an old van (wants to inherit Dad's someday bitchin' camaro)

Dad

‣ Listens to classic & punk rock: Rush, Aerosmith, AC/DC, Queen, The Eagles, Sex Pistols, The Clash, Ramones
‣ Collects figurines: mostly model cars, Star Trek, and sexy anime ladies

Me

‣ Listens to classic & punk rock: Aerosmith, AC/DC, Queen, The Offspring, Blink 182, "My Own Worst Enemy"
‣ Collects figurines: mostly anything her sexual abuser will buy to manipulate her into silence

Dad

‣ Smokes cigarettes (and joints) in private, blowing wisps out the window, preoccupied with the vision of a better life
‣ Caretaker of suicidal wife, financial illusionist, dissembler of shame
‣ Smiles wide, pretends everything is going to be OK

Me

‣ Sucks on candy cigarettes, too cool for school, packing pounds like balloon animals around her waist, armor to survive
‣ Caretaker of younger siblings, wrists covered to secret away the scars
‣ Smiles wide, pretends everything is going to be OK, yesterday's child already jaded, vacant inside

When I Tried to Come Out at 15

"There is no such thing as bisexual—
only trisexual—because you'll try
anything."

— A "dad joke" and implication of promiscuity
pleasantly delivered by my father.

Dear Evil Step-Mother,

You promised my father you didn't need a caretaker;
you assured him. Yet several weeks after the wedding,
everything shifted. I never knew what was real with you:
you flipped from eager fiancé to woeful wife in an instant,
expecting him to work and care for you and the house and
the kids and...

I.

Do you remember how many times you chased
me, my teeth chattering, to the stairs? Ear-splitting
screaming—"Ungrateful! Ungrateful little girl!" The seething
resentments you spit in my face?

One night stands out for its absolute absurdity—Before
heading out for work, Dad told us the dinner plan—takeout
sandwiches. I was on the phone with my friend who made
the most splendid hoagies I'd ever had—perfect ratio of
oil and vinegar, thick mayo, extra extra extra extra black
olives—a sub so superb, I was spoiled rotten. I asked if
she was working. "No." Being a 15-year-old girl validating a

16-year-old girl's shitty job at a fast food place, I affirmed, "Well I don't wanna come if you're not there." I would never affront my father's fortune of Subway for dinner. However, instead of listening to my reasoning, you yelled from the bottom of the stairs after surging at me until your throat was burnt toast, your trembling fingers threatening to wrap around my neck, snuff me out for being such a brat.

II.

When my sister and I were teens, you wrote a letter, handwriting shaky. Placed it on the table where we did our homework for us to find. It said: "I am a human being who lives at 73 North [Redacted] St, too." The letter explained that if we left any more of our belongings in the living areas, they would be left outside in a box to be taken. Certainly, one way to solve a problem.

III.

You called me terrible for tasting my blood on a razor's edge, said *'Didn't I know how much it hurt my father?'* while you stood in the hallway with balled fists, gauze on your wrists.

IV.

The last time I saw you when I was a teen, your body barred my way, demon wings splayed to trap, delaying my ability to get outside to breathe while you berated me. *Just breathe.* You screamed in my face for existing. I hid in my room often, thankful you couldn't make it up the stairs—at least that meant I'd be safe until hunger got the best of me.

Later, I learned you did the same to my sister in her 20s. She needed to escape another screaming speech about never being a "good enough" live-in maid. She should be doing more. More. MORE. You chased her, too. She was forced to flee in the face of your rages, sneak into the kitchen after midnight for sustenance.

V.

When my sister and I finally stumbled upon the definition of weaponized incompetence, it was like the sun rose, illuminating all the shadows where Simba shouldn't go. Your inability to do basic things like make phone calls or read paperwork was believable before we let ourselves see how capable you were with crafting guilt trips, manipulations, lies, and topic shifts when someone neared figuring you out.

After my father's death, you projected your made-up cruelty on me. I continued to stay present with compassion. Beet red boiling rage huffed out through my nostrils, I became Holy Saint—washed away the desire to hate you. Remembered, you're hurt, too.

Yet all you could see through my efforts was an attempt to take everything when all I want is *nothing*.

The Vegan Trinity

between the repeated use of my body and my first rape, i realized i loved animals; they did not deserve our assault, consumption of their sacred flesh. how were they any different from us? just because we cannot understand their language does not mean they are lesser creatures.

they had feelings, bodies, mind, souls. i had all the same. we were kindred spirits, seen the same by society: as things to be fed upon.

no more, i said. my mid-teen mind had figured out an essential truth about myself. i came to my father and his wife not with a request, but a statement.

i was still recovering from butter knife cuts and pink pills, but at last i was ready to take care of myself. i announced "i want to eat plants, not animals."

instead of respecting my integrity, my father and stepmother decided my feelings didn't matter. that choosing not to eat meat was an affront to my father's hard work—his hard-earned contributions.

they shared their decision by refusing to buy me anything but:

~~spinach~~
~~sesame salad dressing~~
and ~~"Oriental" flavored ramen~~

the fridge filled and brimmed over with blue-lipped gallons of 2% milk, sliced processed cheese, yogurt with the fruit i wanted at the bottom, browning burger patties, thick-cut apple-smoked bacon, chicken cordon bleu, frozen veggies already coated in butter.

so, i ate salad and Maruchan noodles for my meals, confused as to why suddenly foods i was allowed to eat before alongside the flesh of my fellow animals (potatoes, fruit, rice, other vegetables) were suddenly banned, and i was limited to those three "acceptable" items.

willfully, my caretakers waited to see how long it'd take until i crumbled and accepted the more important truth: the abomination was not animal slaughter but rather, the concept of the right to choose.

i choked down the fear-filled flesh, chased it with something sweet, and shut my mouth around the raging howl of injustice.

More Unsolicited Fatherly Advice

Suck in your gut, girl.
Start doing crunches.
If you wanna pay for college,
you're going to need a flat
stomach so the men at
Hooters will give you
good tips.

That's the key to success.

What if, instead—
I love my body,
rolls and all, and
you supply
the support
you promise
every time
we speak?

The Cost of Not Believing

I was Daddy's girl until I was stolen.

One night, the shadows and stars
spider leg climbed up my labia:
I became a new "daddy's" girl.

(No, the Reaper never made me call him that.
He wanted me to use his first name like a partner,
a wife. I was mistaken many times for his young
bride between the ages of 11 and 12. Could I have
possibly looked old enough for no one to question
why a man nearing 40 was clinging so close to me?)

He thanked my father for letting us come to
stay with him, even if the words scraped from
his throat still sticky with my blood.

This werewolf, man before others,
beast under my moon, worked his way
under the window I'd shut, prying at the sill
with promises of divine masculine energy
to soothe my separation.

He was saved by Christ.
This was a church sanctioned invasion of
my femininity in God's name.
After all, one must simply proclaim
Jesus their Lord and Savior;
thus the permission slip is signed for
unlimited access to Heaven
in the form of my innocence.

When I broke into fevers,
an inner defense to keep hungry hands from my hips,
I hallucinated Lego blocks falling to crush me.
I sobbed, begged for Daddy to find me,
unbury my shattered skeleton,
glue my broken doll body back together.

Then, the monster-man would creep back in,
check on me, pull at my puppet strings to
make sure I'd not gone anywhere,
not sang the song of my sorrows, not
poured out the secrets sewn in my sinews.
His claws traced my thighs,
hungry maw opening to take me in.

When finally I unstitched my mouth to speak,
my mistake was expecting a bitter misogynist
would value a girl-child's word,
even if she were "*his.*"

I discovered the demon made a pact with my father.
One to undo my Lilith-Mother.
Chop her head right from her shoulders.

A recording device, stealthily hidden among ceiling tiles
tracked calls between my mother and me, the monster
listening to my secret confessions and laments, turning
my torments into bullets aimed to kill any chance I'd
be taken seriously, even by my own father.

The cost of him not believing was all of me that remained.

He Who is God

Our Father who art in Heaven—
and Head of Household.

Father who art Greater than any other.

Father whose word is law.

Father, flickering between sky and sunk into couch.

Father, Man who owns the world.

Makes no mistakes.
Owes no apologies.
Almighty.

Please Believe Me

My own father didn't believe me
own father didn't believe me
I was raped and molested
father didn't believe me
he didn't believe me
didn't believe me
dn't believe me
n't believe me
How dare he
t believe me
believe me
elieve me
lieve me
ieve me
so fuck
ve me
e me
you
me
e

Fall From Grace

What was the original sin that sealed the
karmic contract for our family—the commitment for
every generation to be spoon-fed trauma? Drama.

Was it when underage Mom dated adult Dad,
or the ravenous wretches who abused her until she
normalized seeking attention from older men?

Dad's drug, money, and porn problems?

Mom's affairs?

Dad's lack of fucks to give and finances to fuel them?

The miscarriages—were they a sign?

Was it the smoking? Drinking?

Bipolar Disorder?

The ancestral incest or modern molestation?

Closets full of memories stored in shoeboxes?

If I could pinpoint the origin, the epicenter,
the hotbed for our hell, could I atone for it
by way of ritual sacrifice?

Open another wrist
like peeling back layers of tissue paper
to find the reward within?

Say the right words to break the curse
by not speaking the truth ever again,
tucking it behind a silent wall?

Say a prayer like sucking out the poison.
Conceal the wounds covering our inner angels,
clipping wings.

Peace will come one day.
Not in the form of living through
each blow, and rising again,
but in accepting that as a child,
I had no control over any of this,
none at all.

In My Defense

I had not seen my Father much since
returning to Maryland—
Not once over the four years of undergrad when
he repeatedly called to tell me he'd help out financially.

I'd graduated by then, in more ways than holding a degree.
I wore badges of trauma like pride.
Selling my body to make enough money to pay rent.
Three years battling alcoholism.
A loveless marriage.
A dead daughter.

A certifiable adult now.

So, as I sat across from Dad on the edge of my rickety
childhood bed, I expected us to speak together like two
adults, wizened by our time apart.

"I love you," Dad says from the musty computer chair.

I think: *OK, good. I love you, too, Dad.*

"And your sister," he says, widening the space between us.

Well, of course, we're your daughters.

"But," he says, lifting his feet to spin on wheels.

"But"? How can there be a but?

"I love your sister more,"

*I didn't know this was a competition,
so, thanks for finally telling me the score.*

"You're too much like your mother. You're a cheater, like
her..."

No, I think, my tongue numb. A*ctually, I'm polyamorous—
my partners have always known about each other.*

"And you look and sound like her. I can't look at you without
seeing her, and that's too painful."

*Doomed to fail upon conception.
Let me just cut out my vocal cords,
wear a mask of Vana White so I can silently,
prettily be on screen without bringing up the
things you could have worked on in therapy.*

But, I say none of this. I only smudge a thumb coated in ink
over the story of reunification I'd begun writing.
Shove my self-worth in my back pocket and
sit on it as I drive home.

Breaking Point

Void ink marks the pages on either side of this story,
except the part where I cry alone on the long ride home
because of the way I look, talk, and who and how I love.

I have failed to defend myself in any of the above.

subject: Personal letter, nsfw

from: [Daddy's Girl]
to: [Dad]
date: Sep 13, 2013, 3:26 PM
mailed-by: gmail.com

Dear Dad,

I just want to get some heaviness off of my heart. Let me preface this by saying that I am not asking for or expecting a response, I'm not trying to hurt you, nor do I want or need you to try and "fix" things. I am as I am and have accepted that, but nevertheless, I hope it will relieve me to express these feelings.

I'll try to keep this short. When I was 8 or 9, however old I was that I moved to Maryland, I was broken-hearted. Despite not having a great relationship with you since you worked, and I respect the need for hard work as I do it every day, you were still my father and I loved and depended on you. Many nights in MD I cried, feeling like I no longer had a father because you were far away and my young mind could not rationalize what I was going through. My desire to have a father figure contributed to a complex series of future life events.

I was so excited to come see you in the summers, and when I ultimately moved to NY when I was 15, I thought it would be a good thing for me. We know how that went - ultimately, I was broken by your belief in my abuser over me when it came to my sexual abuse history, and despite you turning that around, it wounded me for a long time.

Our relationship after that point obviously slid downhill, and that is to be expected, given the tension between your wife and I, the circumstances surrounding my abuse, and many other factors. My actions caused others to feel hurt, disappointment, anger, and so on, but I was true to myself and never meant to cause any of those feelings.

After those events, we talked less and less. Every time I did talk to you, it was about money and what awful thing my mother was doing to you now, and ultimately, I didn't know what to do. I felt sorry for you, but also deeply abandoned. Why did my own parent not reach out more often and see how things were in my relationships? Work? Life? How is my health? Instead, you'd occasionally see how I was doing and then remind me that you'd send me money when you had it - something I never cared about. Money is nice, but what I wanted at the time was a relationship with my father.

Last summer when I came to visit you and you told me I

was basically too much like my mother to get along with, that was essentially the final nail in the coffin. I decided at that point that I did not want to pursue a deep father/daughter connection with you because I didn't want to cause you discomfort, and knowing that you were plagued by my resemblance to my mother did not do anything positive for my self-image.

Now that my sister has moved up there, I have been made to understand that you "got what you wanted." It's come to my attention that when I was 8 or 9 and my sister was 4 or 5, you wanted to keep her with you and send me away with Mom. This statement of intent has only served to hurt me more and confirm the fact that I shouldn't be trying to pursue a relationship with you.

I understand, logically, that this has nothing to do with me the person, but your own personal history. I don't think I've done anything wrong by existing, and I'm hoping that in some way, writing this letter to you can get me some very much-needed closure, and hopefully you, too.

I regret that we did not have a better relationship, but I hope that for as wounded as we are, you can have a great relationship with my sister and inspire her to be greater than she is pushing herself to be. I love my sister and worry about her, but she has reached a stage in her life where she needs to learn on her own. No matter how many mistakes I've made, it doesn't matter what I tell her - she won't believe until she's seen it for herself.

I'm not asking you to respond, to call, or anything like that. I don't even know that I want you to, given the hurt surrounding everything. Again, I just hope that me knowing I've said my piece and closed this difficult, damaging chapter, that I can move forward and attempt to regain some of the self-confidence, esteem, and image I've lost over the course of the last several years for believing myself not good enough. I understand that your opinion of me is that I am a good person and that I am doing good things, but I also understand that I am too much like my mother and that wounds you. I'd like us to stop wounding each other through tense and tentative attempts at having a bond, and seek peace, balance, and love in our lives where it is most positive for us.

Thank you for the wonderful things you have done over the years to encourage me and to support me. I acknowledge all of those things and am deeply thankful for them, but I don't know that we are at a stage where we can create a safe, loving light to hold one another in while still trying to communicate. I honestly don't know. My partner is worried that this letter will only serve to cause me more pain if I get rejected. That's why I need you to know that I do not expect or even want a response to this - because I don't want to live in the world of expectations as I have for the past 24 years.

It is not at all my wish to cause you harm - but, you told me how you felt about me, and so I needed to tell you how I felt, too. I love you dearly, but I understand that sometimes despite our blood, things just hurt too damn much to do anything about. I'd like to close the chapter of hurt and find peace in understanding that our complex histories make it difficult for us to relate. I am willing to accept that. I do not want you to try and repair things, only to realize I am still like my mother and that it hurts too much. I want you to know that even if you never respond to this, I forgive you for the way your actions and words hurt me, because I acknowledge that it was never your intent to hurt me - only one soul to another expressing feelings in the course of their personal journey.

I hope this can open a new door for you. I hope it will serve as a healing blessing for me as well.

Love,
Your Daughter

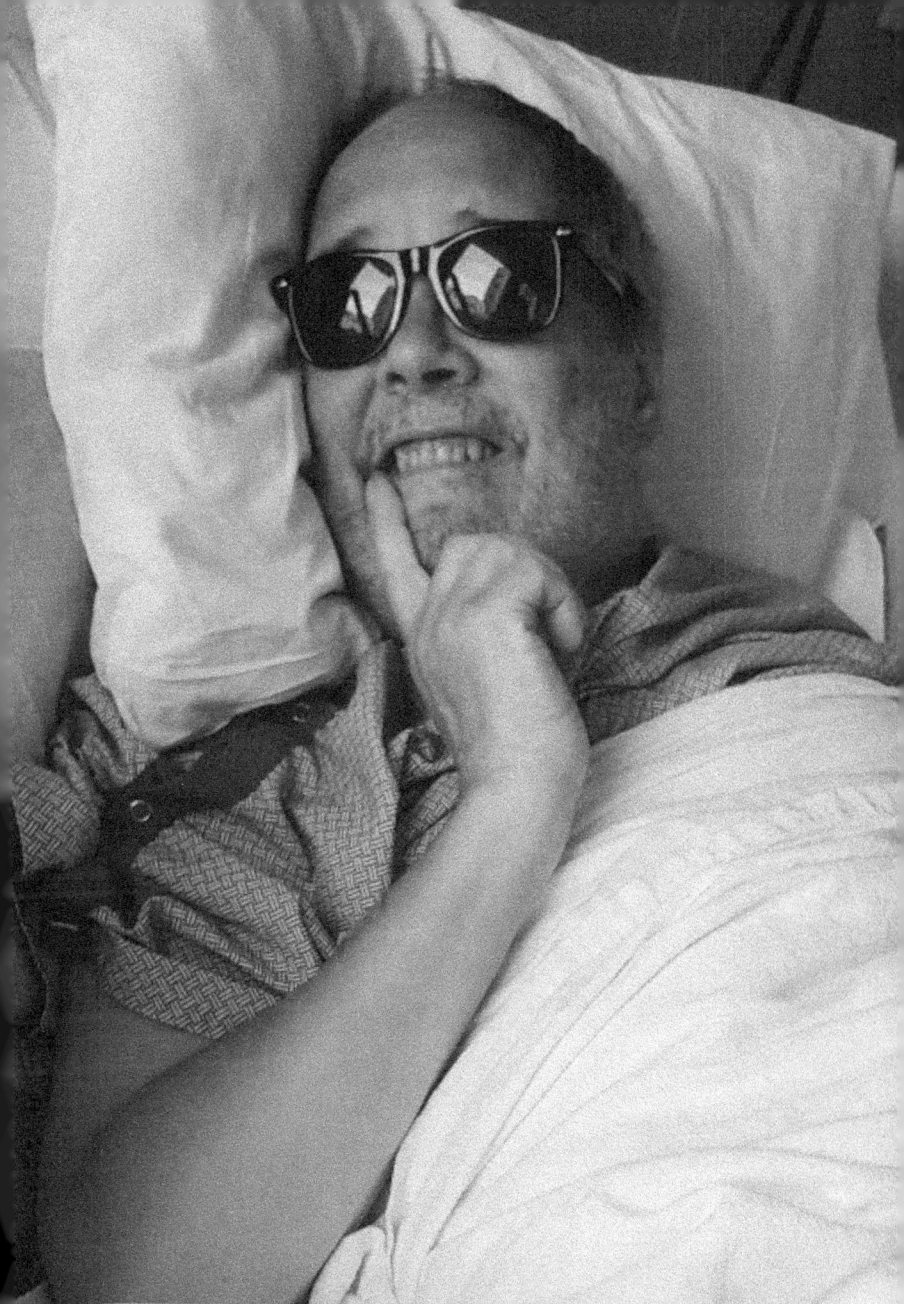

A GRIEF CHAPTER

My Own Toxic Masculine

For two decades, I prided myself in being a hard worker
like Dad, smiling-wide, suppressing the thunderous screams
inside. Ignored the pain that found purchase in every limb.
I had more to do.

Is this why he fell apart?
Why he was always chasing the next high?
I can't blame him.

When you believe the entirety of your life
exists to be the best caretaker you can to
everybody but yourself, eventually,
you have nothing left to give.

By the time the cancerous worm had bit its
way through my father's brain, it was too late.
He could not unmake a lifetime of choices, but
I still had a life to live—nothing so permanent—
just a misaligned masculine mindset ready to be
dethroned.

Every Man I Dated in My 20s

Patterns play out until disrupted—it took me a decade
to realize every man I dated was another face of you:

Nerdy boy with soft eyes or curious mind—
Sci-fi, fantasy, anime fan—with an unrealistic
Ideal of femininity. Patience to a point—
Unless it had to do with me. *I must never change.*
Holes in pockets—unable to get ahead.
Serial collector of some new thing, though.
Add a complicated relationship with pornography.
Amp that up to addiction, maybe abuse.
Layer in an unsavory fetish uncovered too late.
A dash of emotionally unavailable, and certainly
Never listening to my side.

Invisible Insides

Through childhood into my late 20s, I experienced the strangest phenomenon: I was visibly seen, witnessed for the physical form that filled a space—yet unseen beyond the presence of my body—beyond the parts touched, fondled, squeezed—constricted to my ability to be free or low-paid labor, to fulfill a role or duty—daughter, sister, wife, teacher, therapist, healer, surrogate—the emotional labor I provided unacknowledged, my feelings outright ignored or never considered. While I juggled the demands and emotions of two sets of traumatized, projecting parents, I tried to keep my younger siblings safe (+ failed), rapidly made and lost friends from move after move, each bringing more displacement—distraught, innocence destroyed.

Why is it people could see I existed as a container for their frustrations, shames, fears— a place to dump their woes—yet never think to ask about mine? Could it be that somehow my inner worlds have disappeared from the maps, dissociated into obscurity? Could I really be surrounded by people without capacity to witness other's wounds?

Sex Work and Simply Pasta Salad

In my adulthood, poverty looked like:
— Simply Pasta packets every weeknight, doing sex work as
a pro-Domme to make ends meet, simultaneously managing
a full-time plus load of credits for my English-Education
double major, pagan potluck food on weekends and
holidays, white wine, vodka, schnapps
— weeping because my daughter was dead, along with my
dream for a different life; wondering how we'd survive once
I lost access to WIC
— spending every cent I make in surplus, scared of scarcity,
perpetuating the cycle
— the same five professional outfits on rotation for nearly a
decade, bought by my mother on a credit card when I was
starting my teaching internship—could no longer get away
with band t-shirts, baggy pants
— not knowing what it's like to have a day off anymore, only
the faintest memories of a childhood before abuse piled
upon abuse and I lost myself, missing summers of silence
— despair, yet determination—voice shuttering in my
throat, nearly ready to be released

If My Daughter Would Have Lived

At 23, I sit alone on the floor of my 2-bedroom apartment, back pressed against the barren primer-painted wall—sigh.

How wrong (and right) it is to feel relief that my daughter is dead because her own father admitted he'd molest her if she'd lived to see her teens?

If my daughter had lived, the beast that put his fangs in her frail neck would not have risen, some Reaper phantom of my problematic past. He would have been in her house—a lurking leech ready to drain her of her innocence.

I push up from the wall after letting myself float away from my body awhile—balloon head bobbing to this sorrowful song that, thank God, will never be sung.

The curse on this family ends with me.

She's Got Daddy Issues

Packed within just four simple words are:

- tearful goodbyes every summer our family is split in two

- my childhood maple rent with a splintering ax in my mind

- paralysis as my new father figure fingered and fondled my flat chest night after night, while I wept at missing you, desperate for a man who barely looked at me

- stilted weekend phone calls, fleeting holiday visits, and a promise to "buy" my love when all I wanted was your time

- seeking your protection by running back to you, leaving my mother and my life behind, when the sexual misuse of my fragile child's body got to be too much

- finding you would not protect me, but rather scold my bloody wrists while your wife cut hers in bed the next room over; why be silent with her pain and punish me for mine?

- swallowing like a fat egg the "fact" I must not be bisexual, because you said with such finality "there is no such thing." is this why you didn't see me? could never acknowledge a unicorn like me could exist?

- *"choosing"* to be anally raped by the boy that pushed me down and gave me a moment to beg because you and your church told me vaginal virginity was sacred

- you grounding me until I was 30, removing my entire connection to the world beyond the school where my rapist resided, because you found out about my older online boyfriend, only acknowledging he was 6 years older, the same age difference between you and mom, not that he was the first male in my life (other than you) who hadn't sexually used me

- finally, my tongue fizzy and numb, admitting my mother's second husband had molested away my sanity, sloughed off the skin I cut away, only for you to say I was making it up

- listening to you side with my abuser over me and my mother because my mother is a lying selfish bitch and I'm just covering up my own misdeeds

- fleeing, door racketing shut against the protection you'd never given me, starting a life where I'd just give up on myself like my idol did

- losing my virginity not on some holy night, but on a paisley couch to the glow of a digital clock, red like my virgin price

- at minimum 15 blowjobs given to strangers on the first "date" because I just wanted a man to like me for something I was good at

- drunken nights in undergrad, leaning against walls to make it to bed, wondering if I could ever make you proud

- dragging on cigarettes, wondering what the allure was, throwing away health because who the fuck cares

- having a dissociative break from domestic violence and assault at the hands of my love bomber boyfriend at 23, barely three-months fresh off losing my baby. calling him daddy as I fractured inside out

- offering you the wholeness of my identity, only for you to toss that gift away, a crumpled love letter from the child I never got to be

Wrapping Paper Girl

Very few care about the giftwrap or the box.
It is a momentary fixation, a flashy thing,
Full of glitter, pops of color fit for a holiday.
The present within is what they seek, the
Container quickly forgotten once the perceived
Gift is excavated from its confines.

Tossed aside, the parcel or paper, ribbon, tags,
Their best hope is to be recycled, upcycled,
Given a second chance at life before being
Sent to the trash, never to be admired again.

After Seven Rotations
Around the Sun

Peace for many years
between my boundaries and
your calling for help.

An awakening
of Daddy's Girl eternal;
cries out with longing.

Perhaps, it is time!
You will see me in my truth
and find me worthy.

I hope for a hug,
a word of solace, and thanks.
Instead, I am pulled

back into my role
of eldest daughter, always
in charge of the mess.

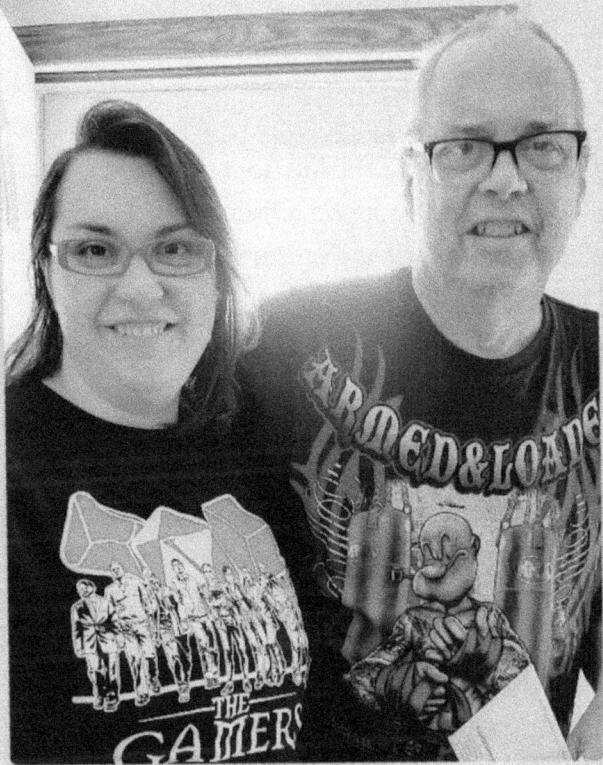

Last visit before Dad's decline –
prepping the will

Cancer Timelines

2013—the same year I cut off my father. I get a primer in brain cancer—it draws the life from a person, a parasite draining all vitality. I support a friend from church while she witnesses her husband's torturous trickling away. By the time I meet him, he's already vanished, a specter barely tethered to his body. I take him a white candle carved with healing runes. He passes overnight, swift as snuffed-out altar flame.

2018—still estranged from my father. I'm contemplating how to leave my Love Bomber. Our worlds intertwine like overgrown cancerous vines, draining support systems that can't sustain us both forever. When things get worse at home, a mutual friend, my Buffle, suggests I move in with her, free myself from the necrotic growth where it festers. Says she and Love Bomber can still be friends, so long as I am safely rooted. I agree. A flash—so soon after she makes the offer, headaches split her open. They find the tumor shortly after the pattern emerges. Our community rallies—healthy foods—meditations—elaborate rituals—all while seeking solid medical solutions. Improvement ebbs, her shoreline sickening with time. Nothing sticks. One evening, she shares with me a vision that's shaken her—a beautiful blue stag in the woods—her harbinger of fate. I watch her self-ness slip from behind her eyes. She becomes a ghost at her kitchen table. Follows the deer to her death. Gone soon after.

2019—an awkward drive-by dinner with my dad. He, step-monster, sister, me, the Lover Bomber, and my now wife meet at a BJs Brewhouse for some of the most eerily dissonant hours of my life. He has his stroke 6 months later—precursor to the cascade of cancers.

2021—the situation with the step-monster reaches critical. Squalor, nothing healthy left in the household. Dad reports, remarkably cheerful, he's recovered from lung cancer, but there's a bigger growth in his brain. Without faltering, but fully triggered, I drive to New York to help him figure out his final will and testament, a side quest to the main mission of breaking my sister out of bad. He chauffeurs me around from Red Lobster to the bank to CVS, telling me how my sister's gonna be fine; she's grown exponentially while living with him. He's proud of her. Still angry at Mom for All She'd Done™. I stay silent, hold a dignified space for him to share his side one final time. He's hospital-bound less than two months later. Dead in three.

Another Life, Another Dollar

You used to call — maybe once a month.
　　You'd talk about money,
　　always, 100% of the time, money.

You'd gone bankrupt,
　　　　　　or
you'd come into a little extra green.
One of two extremes.

Finally, you'd help me pay for school,
Oh, you got a new car, it's so cool,
You've got a shiny new Fender guitar
An upscale, fine-dining dish to enjoy.

When you got sick, it hurt to see how it *excited* you.
A sudden brightness to your sepia eyes,
　　Your voice betraying your relief at being forced to
　　Quit working.

Disability + social security + retirement—
At LAST you were living the "good life,"
a "rich man's life."

(Ordering take out daily,
    leasing another brand-new sedan,
    buying an engine red Mustang
    to store in the garage.)

But, did you really get to enjoy it?

Moments from breathing your last, you call me.

Why?

To talk about money. To make sure I know
    "At last I'll be taken care of." That you threw
    your life away for 40 years to make sure we'd be
    provided for.

I'm nauseated when I recognize that in two years,
I can make more money than you killed yourself
over to put in an account for me and my sister.

The Daddy's Girl in me, buried a lifetime ago,
wrenches herself out from the grave of lies you left her in.
Maple leaves crinkle, peel, falling from her filthy flesh.
Daddy, she cries, *I just wanted your love, never your money.*
I wanted for you to say, "I'm proud of you,
You're an awesome person,
I accept you. I believe in you."
And most of all, "I believe you."

Money will never buy me that.

Outpatient Therapy History

The first time I went to therapy, it was because my parents found I'd been damaged at the broad, veiny hands of a friend's brother. He was 24. I was 12. Therapist #1 looked like Miss Frizzle.

My following therapists mainly addressed the ongoing "relationship" with my Reaper ex-stepfather. #2 was a matron with short white hair who told me to marry for money, not love. Never love. I was 15. #3 looked almost the same, but she was softer. Let me make collages out of magazines while I vented about how my mom didn't understand me. I was 16.

#4 and #5 I've forgotten, those years lost to dissociation. The sixth was the tree lady when I was 23. I sought her services when my husband and I split, separating after the loss of our baby girl. Instead of the immense grief I felt, she focused on my need to leave my new abusive boyfriend. Unfortunately, no matter how much she tried, I couldn't see how the stories of him and my childhood abuser were entangled. How they "loved" me in the same way.

I fired her at 24 and fading—found the woman who breathed peace. Therapist #7, whose tiny, once-upon-a-time fighter's hands could cup my kidneys and make me feel safe.
She grew up in trauma herself—helped me process my relationship with my first husband and grieve my child, concurrent with my father declaring he loved my sister more. I wrote my father out and worked for months in therapy to be okay with all the loss.

Saying goodbye and drawing boundaries with the people I loved was getting easier thanks to twice-weekly hour-long sessions with this Buddha in yoga clothes, who smiled with cheeks, eyes, and hands alike. I only left her care when finances became restrictive, and I had to survive in other ways. I was 28.

When I finally left my Love Bomber boyfriend after seven years of domestic violence, I returned to her to tell her of my new life, introducing her to my now wife. I was 30. She hugged me, shedding sacred tears, and said, "I never thought you'd leave him." Her relief washed over me. I took it in. I hadn't thought it possible, either, but she showed me I had the strength to say goodbye, even if we'd never truly said it in the first place.

I found #8 at 32 while struggling with binge-eating my feelings after acknowledging the devastation of those years with the ex. I picked a male therapist in the hopes I could subconsciously address my fear of men. He had an excellent sense of humor, great button up shirts, and specialized in grief. But, I just wanted help with the eating thing.

"Death is easy for me. My Buffle last year," I said. "I cried a few times, but really I'm just happy she moved on from her pain."

We resolved my issues with food around the time I found out Dad was diagnosed with the same illness that took my Buffle. Instead, I talked about intimacy with my wife. I blamed the years with my stepfather and ex, grieving the loss of my sexuality.

When Dad got sicker, I talked about my roommate situation, grieving the loss of a home that felt safe.

I drove out of state to do Dad's Will, but talked about my sister, grieving for the abuse she'd faced from our stepmother.

"I'm fine with it, really," I told my therapist anytime he'd bring up Dad. I felt a quiet sort of nothing. He was already dead to me, after all. I had done the heart work of grieving a whole therapist ago.

I terminated services. Therapy was going no where. I had nothing to talk about anymore. Life was fine. Saying goodbye to people I loved was easy.

Completely effortless.

An Eldest Daughter's Swan Song

The Crimson Swan, who living had no Voice, when Death
approached, unlocked her burning throat. Leaning forth,
she exposed the charred heart nestled within her broken
breast, sighed, sang her first, her last, then sang no more:
"Farewell, my sanity! O Death, come close these eyes! More
codependency now lives, and I'm more Fool than Wise."

A Self-less story arc ending in disappointment: She will
confront her sense of pride and duty—Acknowledge her
failure to protect the ones she loves, the cycle of suffering
still spinning on.

Soon, she will be pulled back into her role as
Family Protector, left with stacks of legal docs,
a list of people to break the bad news to.

Feet paddling, frenzied beneath a calm exterior,
she will die singing this song shoved unceremoniously
down her decayed esophagus—the script of
Eldest Daughter, written on the day of her birth.

Clatter of Voices

Dishes shattered against a wall.

Not reality—

It's a cacophonous clatter of voices,
so violent it transports me to an era
when my relationships mirrored this.

"When you've been married 20 years..."
the stories start. Excuses for toxicity.

Doesn't matter if it's been 20 years or 20 days,
abuse is abuse.

"My wife and I don't argue," I say.

"Just you wait."

Wait for misery?
For a kitchen filled with broken trust,
all the plates thrown out, pottery shattered?

No—I will not live my days upon tense tile floors
hiding the scent of my midnight snacks
in a corner.

I'll live proudly together—or I'll live alone.

The voices around the dining table will be
calm, caring, or there will be no voice but
my own and the cats' meows.

I will not tolerate such noise.

ScapeGOAT

Problem Child who deserves mistreatment,
chased up rickety stairs into cobwebbed corners,
left to anxious shit in a broken bathroom,
porcelain fissured, no throne.

Hidden, locked for days in a bedroom
so hot she could start a greenhouse and simply forage
for the rest of her miserable days.

Problem Child, until it's realized, oh dawning terror,
that she was the responsible one—
greatest of all time at gathering information—
collecting twigs to build everyone else's future nest.

Now you expect her to be the Problem Fixer Child.
Do you fail to see the folly, still?

You were the problem;
she was the child.

The Long Ride Home

I made the trip from New York to Maryland many times as a child, powerless to turn the car around, bail out on bouncing back and forth between traumas—the only difference being who was doing the batting around of my Ping-Pong ball brain.

Many times on the several hundred-mile stretch between my birthplace and my breaking point, I got ill, my stomach communicating my emotions explosively since my words never mattered. While I could keep quiet around the bile bobbing in my throat most of the time, I couldn't help it when the tangible fear of what would happen next swelled beyond my bubble and my tummy turned inside out.

For decades, I feared traveling because my body associated it with feeling sick and stuck—hurtling toward situations where I would be suppressed, subjugated, and tyrannized by traumatized adults. Once it was entirely my choice, I stopped taking trips, never drove more than an hour or two to the next town over. Whenever I thought of being in a car for hours, that ancient bitterness clumped in my throat until I could no longer breathe.

As an adult, I returned to New York of my own volition only once—to buy drums from a man I met at a pagan festival. It was the trip where my father told me he loved my sister more, and I knew our real relationship was over before it started.

Eventually, I had to go back to get my sibling and help Dad set up his will. When things reached a critical point, Dad dying and Step-monster furious at my sister's existence, I got on the road at around 5 A.M. so I could beat traffic—started the trying trek north.

The timeline is hazy—superhero mode engaged. No consideration left for whether or not my nervous system could make the trip back to one of my childhood hells without consequence. It didn't matter. It was time to bring my sister back, break her free from my father's choices, bring her somewhere she could try again like I had to. Our lives a series of tripping over our parent's problems until we realize they're not our own.

While there in my dusty childhood home, my stomach shredded itself like love notes never sent. I dragged myself through days of flashbacks dropping like bombs against the backdrop of my shuttered eyes, pale with what I was witnessing—disgusting, unclean living conditions, countless scents amplified in the stale, hot air clinging to the house. My father talking about money, money, money. My step-mother expecting me to have all the answers. My sister. My sister living like this for how long?

On the return ride, she shared bits of her life over the prior years—the step-monster's continued horrors, her close-knit, often peer-like relationship with our father, how she'd recently left an awful relationship, mirroring much of my first marriage. She played me some angry-femme music, introducing me to artists that would punctuate my own future chapters of processing. Shared her wishes for a better future. As the trip wore on, we listened to a book on eco-activism, how to give a shit about our environment, our collective health. Together, we planted seeds for sisters tending the Earth, each in her unique way.

For once, that long ride home went smoothly—I knew in those moments that both of us were safe, supported, and loved by one another, by the Universe—no sickness to be found in the space between our seats.

A Rebirth Ritual

In the dying days of my 31st cycle around the sun,
my Earthly father granted me a polarizing parting
gift—contrast divinely timed to begin breaking me free from
codependency—an ultra-plasma arrow puncturing through
past, present, future.

Two days before my birthday, I felt the pull. I pushed past
any protests from my partners, locked onto my target—the
hospital where my feeble father lay. If there were one
last chance to be perfect, to set things right, to fix my
father's mistakes, now was the time—the final window of
opportunity to prep the paperwork, set his so-called plan in
motion (nevermind he should have done that himself when
he could).

I set flame to my ribcage in ritual sacrifice of my boundaries
and comfort, drove 288 miles through the sticky afternoon
heat, only to spend hardly an hour at his side. I organized
paperwork, packed boxes, did the duties expected by both
of my rambling mothers. Closed contracts. Kept it together
for everyone.

I even held space for the front desk clerk at the hotel when she asked why I was in town, and I told her my father was dying. Turns out she knew him. She frowned, deep grooves worn in her sullen cheeks. "He was such a great guy to work with."

I smiled sadly at her, knowing just how to arrange my features empathetically, how to act appropriately in every moment. I swallowed down the truth I'd share if I didn't care so fucking much about what everyone thought.

I wish he'd been a great guy to live with, grow up with, look up to. Wish he'd taught me some lessons not routed in -isms and unwavering independence. Wish he'd given me something other than the occasional cool Dad. No safety. No acceptance. No love once he saw my mother in my eyes.

There would be no delicate dance of death and rebirth for me. Only glorious, rapturous Soul returns, messages written in charcoal made from my own burnt rib bones. Radiant revival rendered in shadow alchemy and pain—I would one day be a phoenix in the form of a butterfly.

Grief

Grief, its chords
     tangled yarn
all
                  o v e r
tight, choking
         my heart
the Ĉ þ ä õ Š

anger

        my mind

bargaining

            denial

is there any reason to this?

Sorrow   my spirit broken in
            rolling
              waves
                sobs

If somehow I
straighten out
these ripples,
can the process
move on in
orderly lines?

Maybe escape,
        maybe lifelong regrets

        ~~Acceptance~~

Grief begins fresh
        as soon as I think its   over.
.ɹǝʌo   sʇi ʞuiɥʇ I sɐ noos sɐ

Fresh ball of yarn unneeded.
It's easier to knot something familiar.

Throat tight,
choking.

swamp brain

Neck strains,
          my bowling ball,
                    giant crystal orb,
                              full of worry head
b
  o
     w
        i
           n
             g

my spine until it might just sn / ap.

The exhaustion settles —

s
i
n
k
s

into tender bones

like concrete
replacing
the marrow.

Heavy. Too heavy.

I'm submerging in a reeking
swamp of sorrow,
agonizing
over questions
I'll never have answers to.

Perhaps,
as they say,
that's for the best —

the
WEIGHT

of such answers would likely be the tipping point
between keeping this head on my shoulders, or
letting it
drown
in the bog.

Happy Birthday

At least you got to wish me a Happy Birthday:
10 seconds of a call before once more,
I lose you in the rant and ramble
about the vampiric beast who has at long last depleted
the last of your resources,
the monster who has destroyed your life.

She took the joy right out of my special day,
no surprise. *[My mother—the one I'm so alike—
was sometimes too independent—like me.
So, sure... It's easy to make me the enemy.]*

But, this leech, this step-monster
this overstayed-her-welcome,
parasite, not symbiotic,
just draining, has ripped this family apart
with her blood-soul-sucking.

Why didn't you try to remove her?
Certainly, there are tweezers for pests like this;
vats of alcohol to drown them in, too.

Bitter

bloody tongue starts the day,
teeth clenched around a stone egg—
a seed of bile resting pursed behind my lips
trying hard not to come out

but it will and does, with every coughing fit,
each vibration felt through the floor, another
message telling me I've got a new responsibility.

this chilly cloak, mantle of numb, doesn't suit me,
granite grey like the rock between my chattering teeth
but it's the only garment I've been given to wear

no matter how I try to scoop it all up,
melt a chocolate in my mouth as a palate cleanser,

I can't chase down the bitter aftertaste of history.

Repetition

As a small child,
    Mom would tell me to do It (Whatever *It* was)
over and over again, as if rehearsing for the play of life
was the most important thing I could do.

I needed to be sensational, land all the roles she didn't—
so second-guessing myself became as effortless,
    thoughtless as breathing.

Now, as I amble through my role in this particular
performance—The Eldest, Handler of All Things,
ever with a fake smile plastered to keep up the Picture of
Perfection without Restraint or Resentment—
    I can't trust I'm the lead character.

    I exit stage right to observe.

Between the curtains, the Evil Stepmother cackles,
    mighty in her second role as Wife.
She sees the roles of Daughters as less important—
    will ensure she announces this every time we take five.

My Sister huddles in the background, trying to hide behind
props and scenery, hoping she will be spared some misery.

My Mother shakes a stack full of papers,
nearing the edge where I cannot permit myself to go.
The spotlight swivels, threatening my secure position.
I quickly climb to the catwalk, desperate to escape the
lines she delivers at me. I know they will keep me here
    forever if I am not careful.

Dad, King of the Show, dressed in a Jester costume,
strolls onto center stage laughing. Laughing.
He stands above the trap door—we all know
    any moment he will escape beneath it,
      lost from our sight forever.

I'm more ready than I think.

Ready to sweep the actors from the stage—
attempt to find myself amidst the heaps of costumes I've
been forced into.

My role is not to repeat the performances acted out
    by my parents.

I am meant to be the protagonist in my own
    grand production.

Top 10 Qualities of Parentified Daughters

Parentification: when a child is forced into a caregiver role for their parental figure(s), responsible for adult emotions and decisions from a young age.

Parentification may lead to:

10 – a meager understanding of boundaries, having had no personal space, no room to care for their own needs

9 – overidentification with "obligations," self-reliance, fierce independence

8 – challenges with expressing vulnerable feelings, suffocating in "strength," unsure how to seek support

7 – perfectionism, plain and simple

6 – being seen as "very mature for their age," the loss of their childhoods celebrated

5 – a compulsion to save others rooted in unstable family systems and constant upheaval

4 – early or risky sexual behavior (often layered with grooming and outright abuse)

3 – resentment dosed in guilt—never able to meet the multitude of mandates placed in their already weary arms

2 – a sense that trust is as ephemeral as the fae, a figment of fantasy, something out of reach beyond the veil

1 – an inescapable need for approval tangled up in expectations they never agreed to

It takes compassion, openness, and an unrelenting desire to see your Self beyond the limited scope your "superiors" projected on you. Ready to disengage from the seemingly endless cycle of generational dramas? Shadow work can stop these symptoms from spreading further.

You don't exist to please your parents.

I know it's possible to escape the leaden words your Elders used to build your cage. One day, after years of arduous ascent towards *better*, I was blessed to wake into a life where my People-Pleaser Part was no longer puppeteering the show. The stage for my story had transformed, now an infinite backdrop of diamond stars and spirals, my soul a comet streaking toward unfathomable pleasure and peace.

Peace, Without Me

What would you do without me?
Your cry, "Foul!" Say I'm like my mother,
forget all the ways I'm exactly like you.

Falling apart—can't hold me up,
yet I manage to hold everyone else's weight,
somehow. Sound familiar?

No wonder as soon as I'm out of tasks to do
I find myself awash with angry tears against
bloodshot whites, drifting, beyond exhausted.

That's you, too; even as you lay in your hospital bed
dying, you're still trying to juggle the world,
make sure it's all taken care of—trying to make sure
I'm set up for success when you finally go,
ready to pick right up where you're leaving off,
collecting everyone else's scattered pieces.

I don't have the heart to tell you no.

[NO.]

Because all I ever wanted was to be a Daddy's Girl,
your mini-me.

Here, now, I'm just like you once more.

Tired.

Hope fading.

Devastation flows through my "perfectly healthy" blood—
I wonder why no one can see how much I'm suffering—
can't understand why my entire body is alight with magma,
my flesh tender to any touch.

Why can no one see I just want to shut my eyes?
I want for me exactly what I want for you.

Peace.

Immune

Every part hurts,
From lower back and hips
To neck and shoulders,
Aching, piercing throbbing,
Flashes of red along my spine.

My mind hurts, too
Each thought a new
What If
Torture.

It has been three days since
I saw your weak body curl
Like a spiral straw—
Upper body all wound up
Upon itself
Lower body straight,
Outright
As if any moment you might
Leap from this life.

You said, "I'm ready to see what's out there."
"Get yourself a spaceship," I offered.
"Be your own spaceship," my sister counter offered.
"Yeah..."

Could you be ready to rocket off into
Worlds you've dreamed of since you were a boy?
A grown man with collected figures of the
Starship Enterprise

I'm not immune from that same sense of wonder,
Nor, it seems, from sharing in your dying pain—
My empathy so often a gift betraying me
Letting me live as if in your place,
Trying through your torture to so much as lift my
Own head. The ability to see through other's eyes
Allowed me to dismiss my hurts in favor of some
Cosmic Truth—some purpose for this suffering.

They say you have to go on living for the dead,
But he isn't dead yet.

Does this mean I must live like the dying do?

Find me a spaceship, then, because no one
Should have to live in this much pain. I will
Soar through the sparkling stars with
Diamond rays piercing through the windows,
Right into my worthy Soul.

to be mortal.

your voice is dried leaves. sticks stuck in the throat,
too sharp to be dislodged without damage

you speak of nightmares—floods, water rising above
your knit brow; not enough money in the account—
your parched words rustling out raw and caustic

you are scared, I see. the end comes uncertainly,
glints of clarity like crystal runes cast across
the Universe, too distant to discern.

nothing makes sense. there is no
means to this end that could ever
soothe your battered bones

if I could build you a refuge,
a pyre to lay your body on,
I'd let the earth carry you through

but, I am not a God that walks
these lands. I am just your daughter
weeping roughly into her open hands.

My Last Phone Call With My Father

"I can't think I can't think I can't think I'm sorry Nothing makes sense I can't comprehend I'm sorry I just want it to stop I was almost there I was almost there I was almost comfortable No one gets it NO ONE GETS IT no one will let me I am tired of yelling at my wife I am sorry please tell the people here I am sorry I can't think I don't understand I can't think I can't think I can't hear I can't think I can't do it anymore I've cried at least three times today I just want to fall out of my bed and hit my head I'm sorry I'm sorry No one will let me be at peace No one will let me I'm in so much pain I wish I could just beat my head off the floor I'm sorry There's always something I have to get done I can't get anything straight anything I can't think I can't understand I can't hear I'm ready I'm holding up everyone else from their stuff please tell them I'm sorry no one will let me be at peace no one will let me I'm ready I'm sorry..."

Storm

This morning, my head split open like the sky.
The clouds shortly followed. I could not move.
Later, even as I lifted my head, the storm surged on,
the force of the rains washing the
woody mulch and loose dirt down the side of the
hill outside my bedroom window.

Inside, I wept. My own rain was a breaking,
thunderous rumbling of seethe and swell—
of sorrow I never thought I'd feel.
I was so convinced before that when this
time came, I'd be stalwart—a stone.

Instead, I am the tempest beating against
the building. The quake of this unstable
mountainside. I am the undulating tide
of this downpour, rocking in waves, again,
again, wailing like the wind. I am a danger
to myself, and were I less Captain Caretaker,
I would be to others.

In the evening, my head calmed, no longer
pounding with pressure trying to
crack open my core.

But, my heart rages now as the world goes on.
While my father's suffering goes on.
While the unrelenting dagger of a past that
cannot be changed punctures my sternum, and
the questions go on.

Storms pass. I know this ache, too, will
eventually lift, the sun peering through the
silvery clouds, all luminous love, the shining
clarity of my purpose beyond codependency.
But, not now.

In this present rackety breath,
I am the gale in gray, weeping.

On the Edge

A choice must be made in
what *could* be your final hours.

I walk lines through the green,
seeking spiritual wisdom on the wind.
God flows into me. Flows out. In. Out.
Becomes me. Is me. Always has been.

Breathe, beneath breaking canopy, shifting
with sunlight, trickling bend, water flickering
flashes over rocks, citrus scent stickied on my
hands as I savor and share my fruit with the earth.

I ground down, send out tap roots from my feet,
feel the foundation of wisdom beneath me blooming
with my breath—I know no matter what comes,
I am safe, held by Mother Gaia, fully supported as I
find my way through this inky veil of instability.

Angels sing, crowd around my shoulders:
shimmering brilliance through celestial wings.

They're sending Archangel Michael, for you—
he whose namesake you keep as your middle.

All layers in meditation, mediation finally align.
There is no past, present, or future existing
without the others.

No mind, body, heart, nor spirit separate.

I hugged you goodbye. I touched your sleeping
mind and soul with my waking. I spoke to
you from the heart. The journey can now end.

I came to the precipice and chose peace.

Rest.

Saying Goodbye

Sister and I carry you to the healing waters of
the sacred place I saw in my dreams, days before
we came to say goodbye.

A stone building open to the air, pillars holding strong,
secure, rock glistening with flecks of mica in the sun.
A serene spa fed by a silver lake straight from the
breast of Mother Moon, basking in the glow of Father Sun.

Sinking into the water beside you, your youngest
strokes your head as she often did, reminding you—
you are loved. You are okay.

Your eldest, I pull from your chest all the tangled chords
of this life, weaving my fingers in to gently untwine them.

Chanting ancient words of mending, blending
time and space, soul and sense, I urge you
to separate spirit from body.

So many, so heavy the knots, binding you to this life.
I feel all this pain you carried for so long. It leaves me

hoping the lessons you learned will be taken into the
next life, be well kept, need no repeating.

I light the fires, emerald sparking, to burn at the
edges of the strings where they sink into your
weakening flesh with shark teeth.

Be released from this realm. It is okay to move on.

Sister and I lift you from the waters, carrying you to
the great pillar of light—the lift into the upper world
where you'll choose your new incarnation after a time of
blissful respite.

You deserve that, Dad.

Now, though, you have a choice to make.
Suffer. Or be at peace.
We've done all we could do.

Before we part, I call down Azrael, Michael, Raphael—
ask them to take over from here.

Sister and I go to the lift down,
down into our lives where we'll have to
walk the looping paths of grief without you.

Your daughters are ready to say goodbye.
Goodbye, Dad. Goodbye.

AFTERMATH

He's gone.

White Noise

Room filled with warbles—
  tingly-numb arms,
    core taught with tension
a tightrope
  close to
fraying

Walking, waking,
  both are navigating
    sound waves of deceit,
untruths kept in creeping shadows—
twining tendrils of self-doubt,
  tugging until it's
    time to come clean.

I do my best version of a breast-stroke,
  trying to dislodge myself from
    milk thick cobwebs
    sizzling organs,
      stewing me from inside-out
  this flesh cage—

Body & feelings on fire,
    burning, burning embers,
but the brain's just buzzing—
a forgotten
  Fitbit alarm,
gone off under a laundry heap
    so distant,
        so ambiguous

            might as well ignore it.

After all,
  I've got good practice with being ignored.

For now, all I can do is ride the
  ripples of sensory input,
    grasping for the intangible
swish-swashed in with the little bits of reality
    that can be drunk in through fingertips.

I wish my dream had come true—
  that we'd ushered us all to a place
    where none of this bullshit
    remains.

Entangled Lies

In the aftermath of death, fingers stuck to sticky webs,
we try to untangle all these threads. Try to smooth a life
deceived. For Father's fooled us, Father lied.

The story's incomplete, unknown, tripping over tales that
can't be told. His tongue is ashes, dried up luck,
shifting sides with every sigh, and all these lies.

Was he a rich man, a poor man, a Christian, or cheat?
A healer, a conman, or the nicest guy you'd meet?
An enigma, untraceable, a mirage in the heat?
My father has fooled us. My father has lied.

Swindled our step-mother, ran himself into debt,
promised us payouts, but didn't prepare for success.
Said it would be fine, easy, and smooth, yet unfindable
forms and addictions abound; I'm now left wondering
what kind of father I've found—He wasn't a role model;
he wasn't a saint. A trickster who fooled us.
A great man who lied.

Wishbone Pt. 2

I am divided perfectly down the center of my spine:

On my right, in the light is all, I've ever known—
people-pleasing perfectionism, a child learning to
control my place amongst familiar constraints,
losing myself slowly to constant caretaking.

On the left, submerged in silky shadows, something
unknown—the possibility of a life where I fill my
cup first, then overflow, prolific, excavated prismatic
gems pouring into the world around me, freely from
the wide-open portals in my rosy palms.

In the Silence

At Church on Sunday morning, the minister guides us
in meditation. She always gives us a word or a phrase,
something to hold onto while we dive into the waves of our
thoughts, fighting or flowing with the current. Once the
anchor is in place, she takes a step back, whispering an
invitation—
"In the silence...
 In the silence...
 In the silence..."

In my silence, my father's face swims to the surface,
crashing up over the crest of craggy grays and cerulean skies
reflected. His agony glints, a broken blade shattered over
the choppy ocean. I reach for his hand, but he's already
drowned.

He was silent when I was a child, absent from all the
mundane moments—oh, how I longed to make a sound and
be seen.

He was silent when I dared be myself, more than a

photocopy of his preferences, style, beliefs—when his church deemed me inappropriate: 1) for loving camo and black too much, 2) for loving girls, boys, all beings.

He was silent about his wife, my step-mother, while she slit her wrists—bore them like bloody shackles for my sister and I to see—standing dissociated from the spaces where we were screamed at, her horrible voice echoing through the bones of our heartbroken home.

He was silent for years and years while I stumbled, drunk out of high school and into college, paving my way alone, getting by through what I knew: self-destruction. I sold my body. Sipped peaches and cream mixed drinks like cough medicine, begging it to cure me of this sick feeling of separation.

He was silent and unresponding when I asked him to respect the boundary that he not invite one of my abusers, his wife, to my queer wedding—opted instead to miss the event himself, watch later.

In the silence, I witness a thousand fractal paths like rivulets of rain down a foggy windshield bringing streams of clarity where once there was only obscurity. Paths he might have explored, had he opened his mouth to speak, to stand beside his daughter rather than beyond, before, or nowhere near. His silence aches.

And now, it is eternal.

Baked Bravery

When Daddy died,
I inherited his stash and habit.
A hand pipe.
Metal.
Dark blue.
Plastic baggie of street gold
stashed in the bedside table.

I, too, felt I'd found my life and
freedom alive in green.

Willow-wisping away in a black bowl
caked thick with tar, like my foundation
when I was 15 (I looked 25,
my eyes already blank and tired,
glossy obsidian from birth).

When I get high, the rituals flow,
the channel opens wide,
the fear vanishes (or so I tell myself).

Finally, I can express.
Only, I cannot breathe.

In undergrad,
I had vodka and schnapps,
sticky cups collecting courage on my
cluttered desk, drunk and sideways four nights a week.

My stomach ached, acid eating away my esophagus.
There was no denying it was poison.

But, flowing through life feels far better when I
puff, tilt my head back to look at the clouds, and
tell myself this is just medicine.

A Jigsaw (Missing Pieces)

Pinned to the corkboard in my father's office is a photograph of him as a young man, smiling. Although he may never be trusted again, it doesn't matter now that he's dead.

His face is made of smaller images, some undiscernible. Some clear. All attempting to complete a whole.

He presented a particular face to the world, now made muddy by the fragments unearthed as we try to unbury the life he'd lived:

- One half of a couple who never really worked together now wounded to widowing.

- Two adult children, broken from his spell, never again to believe their father merely a simple man trying to protect his family.

- Abandoned his church because they wouldn't pay for his home repairs after a flood.

- Collected stuff like it would somehow collect him decency.

- A few addictions, the remnants of which pile in drawers and cabinets, ashy corners, resin sticky Ziploc bags, questionable DvDs contained in filmy plastic covers.

- A schemer to the core, passing on the art of secret-keeping to his kids, a tradition we'll keep no more.

The mirage of ethical finances dissipating under closer inspection:

- Hundreds of bank statements printed off—ink crisp even with age.

- Stacks of paid bills; stacks of unpaid bills. A toppling tower.

- At least three accounts opened in his wife's name without her consent

- Thirteen checkbooks, mostly balanced, mostly ancient.

- Loan paperwork from three different companies, their purpose unknown.

- Several thousand dollars of mystery debt on unaccounted credit cards.

- A retirement account, blocked from access.

- A deferred comp account to be split between sister and I (already with a loan against it).

- A mystery life insurance policy, shredded by step-mother to her own detriment.

One dilapidated ancestral home, barely hanging by the boards:

- Complete with 1.5 bathrooms (with only one that .5 works).

- Five bedrooms; one livable (though my sister managed, somehow).

- Several broken windows.

- A dust and must-filled basement still damaged from the flood.

- Hundreds of power tools hardly ever touched.

- Three struggling-to-breathe AC units, wheezing in the swelter.

A picture of a life forever incomplete, like
a five thousand-piece puzzle I'll never finish.

Addendum to "Another Life, Another Dollar"

Now, you cannot call.

You are ashes in a box beneath my desk.

I sit in stacks of paperwork unraveling the long con—

In tabletop roleplaying games, we joke about long cons,
imagining a character tagging along in our adventuring party
selling a one sided story only to pull out a surprise stab,
the truth they've been in disguise for years while
we thought they were the dearest bedfellow.

This is a different sort of long con.

I make phone calls, most of them about your money.

You're bankrupt.

It hurts to see how you lived the "good life" knowing you
wouldn't have to sort the messes once you were gone.

Signed every dotted line, fooling us all.

After you're dead and gone, I am left with more questions than answers, the debacle of your constant deception a source of suffering that may remain for the rest of my days.

- Why did you take a loan out against the retirement account meant to go to your wife?

- How is the "inheritance" you "worked so hard for" a sum barely worth the time it takes to fight with all the paperwork?

- Despite making a salary equal to or more than mine for a majority of your late career, how did you "struggle" while your mortgage was 1/4th my rent?

- Your life does not make mathematical sense. How can you only have paid of $11,000 on your $50,000 home in 12 years? How many times can you refinance and get money back, legally, between bankruptcies?

- What the actual fuck did you spend that invisible money on?

In the end,
I accepted I would
never hear you say,
"I'm proud of you,
You're an awesome person,
I accept you. I believe in you."

And most elusive, "I believe you."

But, I hoped, maybe,
the money you would provide in death,
money you promised my entire life,
would be a symbol of your love.

It could help me get a home, somewhere safe.

I'd imagine you were protecting me.

I waited, as if receiving a check one day
would prove at last you loved me...

All this time, I was long conning myself.

In the sweat of thy face shall thou eat bread...

My father's cremains still sit in the box they came in, gray and unremarkable (literally unmarked save for the sticker claiming his name and location of cremation). I've been unable to bring myself to buy him something special, some expensive, artistic piece of ceramic, wood, or metal to house the ashes that are all that remains of his earthly body. A body that made a living taking care of bodies that couldn't care for themselves, but then forgot his blood, his family, those housed beneath his own roof.

In Tarot, the body is related to the suit of Pentacles. Pentacles are related to finances. Finances are related to everything my father fucked up, and well, I've got no mind to give him more of what he, couldn't give— Energy, time, and truth.

He took out my entire savings account when I was a child, promised to pay me back, then never did.
He said he'd check in on my college years, send me a little something to take care of myself, then never did. Forgot my birthday frequently.

In the afterlife, does he look up or down and snicker
about how he got to keep it all to himself in the end?

Standing in his house after he'd passed, I flipped open
a notebook he'd written in, hoping to find account info,
some way to balance his debts. Instead, I found a scribble
in his handwriting, a piece of wisdom he wanted to pass
on to the world: *IF THEy ArE FOOL ENOUGH TO LET
YOU SIGN ON THE DOTTED LINE GO fOR IT [sic].*

When I asked my sister what in the world she thought
this historical record meant, she said, voice bemused:
"Dad lived in the moment and didn't care what
messes he left behind because it would no longer be his
to deal with." Typical. I guess by being born,
we were fool enough to sign some cosmic dotted line
to put up with his bullshit—clear out the rubble he left
in passing us by.

So, the box seems suitable. He's just fine and
comfortable there—no need for fancy.
He pursued that in life, relentless,
often failing to see the ways he was
burning down every other thing around him.
Just ashes to dust, cast from Eden.

Where There's a Will...

Where does what you wanted of me, and what
I wanted to offer start and end? Your
eldest child, ever striving to be Daddy's Girl,
I've somehow agreed to empty myself on your behalf.

Yet, I've only so many spoons with which to
feed myself. Only so much metal to make brackets
to hold myself together. There's light shining through me,
not because I'm some holy spirit, but because I've
worn myself thin from writing down your wishes and
your will on paper made not of your money, but
my skin—each decree stenciled between my
shoulder blades, snaking down my sides.

Why am I trying to build and bulwark your
boundaries when you never could
admit mine existed?

Most days, I don't require thanks for my service. But,
normally those I serve have not bitten me down to my
last crumb.

Meanwhile, you have repeatedly chosen to speak on
whether or not I was worthy, always choosing *not*.
I've waited my whole life for an
atom of acknowledgment from you—
I thought, maybe, before your last breath,
perhaps a little "Thank you for your help"
could be the exchange for my pain.
Still, somehow...

If I help, it means draining my cup. My coffer.
It means digging up everything I took so long to
bury, dredging up the soil that I carefully packed
over weeping wounds. Helping your wife means
hurting myself—which is what ultimately killed you.

Is this the inheritance you left for me?

Step-Monster

If my mouth was made from glass and poured out poisons, I'd open it to give you the trickle of my mind that drizzled through, liquified remains of a brain battered by years of abuse; not just by bumbling men with broad hands and a craving for innocence, but by you, too. Your voice crackling in the air, a whip incomparable to any barb for its sharp precision.

Screeches echoing down the halls between us, a constant reminder that I would never be good enough for my father because you said so. Made it so. Your black magic winding tendrils around his neck made sure no promise would ever be kept again, unless it was to you.

You wonder why your children—both adopted and step—fled the nest at the first chance. Didn't care if their wings were under-formed and they might plummet to their death. It would be better than accepting your motherly "embrace." That touch was akin to crushing, your claws scraping along the facets of our glittering youth, a pile of discarded rubies and sapphires.

I could never get enough space. Where my fill-in-father snatched at my budding sexuality, got too close to the prize I kept in my womb—you, the fill-in-mother, rammed still bloody razor blades into my chest to cut me a new hole to try and breathe from.

I will never reconcile how a fellow survivor could hop so swiftly the next train to "Don't Believe Her" and get off at the stop for "She's Making It Up for Attention" when, at last, I scratched the truth from my sandpaper throat.

Failed to figure out what you gained by slitting open new wounds every Tuesday night with the door cracked. Chased me, your tongue aflame with lithium. Trilling terror. Voice bombastic, blowing holes in my bedroom floor.

We could have been kindred, bound by mutual empathy for anguishes shared, wrongs excavated from the caverns of our "female" bodies. Instead you spoke in feigned ineptitudes. Banshee howling lies. Pushed a constant competition where no contest need be: "You may be his daughter, but I am his WIFE."

I shut my mouth over the words that want to vomit free. Even after years of your vampire fingers puppeteering invisible threads to collect blood in cups, I am not you. I will not slake my thirst for vengeance on another suffering soul.

Silence is my gift to us both.

Nothing I Do...

can save another person from their trauma.

No matter how perfectly I like to pretend I handled
navigating minefields of fucked up adults, I had
no actual measure of the level of manipulation my
elders were capable of—no concept of the methods
they'd use to keep us small, silent, scared.

Years later, I found out my sister wasn't saved.
We suffered in so many of the same ways.

I had to learn the hard way—no amount of self-sacrifice
amounts to anything worthwhile.

It never does.

Obituary

THE POET'S PAPER, Wednesday, June 30th, 2021

Daddy's Girl

Daddy's Girl passed away on June 27th, 2021 alongside her father. He passed from complications with pneumonia on top of his two-year fight with brain and lung cancers. Daddy's Girl died rather painlessly, drifting off into a wakeless slumber, slipping silently between the layers of grief and longing that had crowded her existence for so long. Without the "life support" of never feeling good enough to cloud her inner peace, she simply let go.

She was born on June 6th, 1989 to her father and mother in Pennsylvania. As a child, she strived to impress her father, thinking the ultimate achievement was to be a caretaker like him, providing for the family by poorly juggling multiple jobs and failing to financially plan. Daddy's Girl often dressed like her father, pretended the same cars, music, and games he liked were cool, and did not confront him about how his lackadaisical approach to her abuse history led her to feel worthless and alone. She looked just like him, so she figured following in his footsteps was nature, nurture unrequired.

In the final years of her life, she survived by curling into herself, hoping somehow she could be seen as worthy to be his daughter before she succumbed to her seemingly incurable wounds.

Unfortunately for her relationship with her Father, aging transformed her in ways he found unacceptable: An individual, vegan, fat, Queer, polyamorous, Earth-loving.

Things that came effortlessly to her were argued to be unnatural, but she returned to them repeatedly, her rainbow moth wings fluttering her back to her soul's flame no matter how much it burned at the "family bond."

She is survived by hope, serenity, and gratitude. She was predeceased by false moral guidelines, patriarchal religions, and prescriptions for a life frankly not worth living.

In lieu of flowers, Daddy's Girl can best be memorialized by radical acts of compassion and shamelessness.

Donations of joyful poems, words of resonance, or simply signs of solidarity are gladly received.

Sky Fathers

So much can change in three months, a year, three years, three lifetimes over thirty years. Time is meaningless when I can quantum leap, portal crawl, place myself in anything, everything, all at once. I've gotten good at opening gateways to anywhere I want to go, splitting the space-time continuum, bisecting the triangle of temporal existence to delve into the void between, beyond, everywhere, and all. I weave all my magics in multitudes—blueprint bare for me to see.

There is a chasm between us, Divine Masculine, Heavenly Father. My ego temples have crumbled in a false kingdom of pain—the rift between us, unfathomable, packed with poison, corrupted our container—so let us reconcile this split, once and for all. It is time to build something new from the vast void, zero point where we can vibrate as one.

I stand upon a spiral stair, a comet streaking through the milky galaxy. Held in a beam of golden light, I float in the center of a crimson pentagram, speeding through pitch-dark sky. Arms outstretched, palms lifted, unicorn horn aimed at all the possibilities that will open when I reclaim the mystic marriage within, I proclaim:

YES!—

I am a yes for a loving relationship with the Sacred Masculine structure. Yes to being Flowing Feminine Force. Yes, Solar, Lunar, Earthly, Divine Union between God, Goddess, and I. Yes, fertile fields where I can plant the seeds of new Universes.

YES!—to Life.

I tip my head back and open my mouth to collect the cosmos, the primal power of creation.

My womb blooms with lush vines, red roses bursting, vibrant. My lifeblood spills over in fragrant petals, rubies tumbling from my lips as I sing. The sound of my spirit's song ripples into the macrocosm, impacting each atom it reaches with the sweetness of a soul unleashed.

I am Infinite Inception.

I am the Living World dancing in Shadow and Light.

I am held, Holy.

A Few Notes on New Money Mindset

— Debt is simply an agreement to pay someone else back over time for something we want now. It's nothing to be ashamed of.

— The credit score didn't exist in general until the year I was born (1989). It's just as made up as I am.

— There are many ways to be rich. Instead of spiraling into scarcity mindset, focus on the capacity to hold more resources, like upgrading to the next biggest mixing bowl in the cabinet.

— Decide. Live now, not in an uncertain future.

— Remember, time is money, and money is energy, so put your money where your mouth is and align it with your dreams. They are among the few things that are truly *yours*.

An Ode to Marijuana

I get it now.

When the going gets tough,
just toke, and take it day by day.

In a puff and plume, let worries lift in
billowing clouds, cough out the pain,
dry up the tears that threaten to choke.

Life's too short, so light up.

Powder Keg Profile

It's a chilly Sunday morning in early February. As usual, I doom scroll Facebook from my phone during my bathroom routine. I wish one of my friends a happy birthday, wash my hands, then walk across the house to get on my computer for work.

I pull up Facebook again since I'm in the middle of marketing an upcoming anthology, building my online presence as an author, guide, and newly full-time CEO. A typical weekend as an entrepreneur.

Instead of my profile popping right up, a black box looms over the screen center. My account is suspended. A blaring blue button—Appeal—sits below the barebones explanation of my sudden ban. Mind whirling, limbs numb, compulsory guilt clenches in my gut. What did I do to deserve having my voice and connection shut down, my community scattered like digital confetti? I find my center, avoid exploding in fireworks of fear—trust there's been some mistake.

I click to appeal, convicted in knowing I've done nothing wrong. My recent posts share about healing, recovering from generational trauma, shadow alchemy, and personal work. The screen asks me to verify my identity. I upload a picture of my marriage license and a photo of my face. That's all it lets me do.

Less than 24 hours later, my account is *permanently disabled,* with no appeal available. At least I can download my data, right? No. There is nothing available for me to access except my login information. Security settings. No contacts. No photos. No posts.

This news is a flashbang grenade—I'm blind in a moment, floating in an endless sea of gunpowder gray—confused, disoriented, all sense of self flickering upward, disappearing into the dark. This platform, this program, is my *work.* My primary connection to the world. Where...

Lightning rips through me, my nervous system illuminating horror in a second—*I never downloaded Dad's photos from Messenger. I might never get those pictures back.*

My tears are flint striking steel cheeks. My voice volleys a mortar shell into the Matrix:

I will not be silenced.

Time is a fleeting, formless thing

My 12th summer, I spent my whole weeklong vacation with Dad playing Final Fantasy X on his PlayStation. I panicked when the game guide told me I was only halfway through the storyline, yet I was scheduled to shuttle back home to my mother's house where the Reaper resided in three days. There was something about Tidus and Yuna's story I needed to see through—needed to know before I dissociated once more into my assailant's embrace.

Super-Dad came to the rescue—rented a Game Shark so I could cheat, ensuring none of the characters I'd grown to love could die as I sleeplessly powered through over fifty-hours of a science-fantasy romance. When the credits rolled, I sobbed, seeing myself to my room alone where I could listen to the sparkling symphony of my adolescent heart. While I didn't get the happy ending I wished for, symbolism swirled around my head in spirals, drawing me away to a world without *Sin*—and the possibility of one day meeting a man who would do anything to stop me from sacrificing myself on the altar of the world.

Back in Maryland, I built a shrine to the male lead. Hidden in my wardrobe, an image of his grinning face was pinned beside a permanent marker scribble: *I <3 Tidus*. This boy from Zanarkand was my pixilated beacon of light, born of bubbling dreams, summoned for heartbreak. I was Yuna—longing to hear a whistle of hope from a man who made me smile. Behind hanging clothes, I prayed as the denizens of Spira did for peace from destruction. Prayed for love and laughter. For a miraculous end to my pain. To one day see my eyes light up at the sight of myself in the mirror.

No blessing in the form of a blonde boy found its way to me in a portal overnight—no man swept in to selflessly save me, even after years. All my wishes took new forms—alchemized in the liminal span between my shoulders, tucked behind my sternum for the right time to be realized.

Fifteen years later, I beat Final Fantasy X again—this time without cheat mode. I patiently played through hundreds of hours to unlock each side story and secret, see each map, collect each morsel of lore, more moments and memories with this game that inspired me to live on. I'm no longer running from monsters threatening my peace—I find myself surrounded by support.

I weep for the dreams that have faded—but I will never forget them. They are here in all my wishes coming true.

Unlimited Pancakes

One Summer, I attended a digital self-development retreat.
During a coaching activity, the facilitator asked:
"If you could have unlimited anything, what would it be?"

I blurted out what swelled in my soul: *Pancakes!*

My Ayurvedic Coach once shared my craving for pizza,
braided, doughy pretzels, fresh baked cakes, soft chewy
cookies, was because I hungered for soft, pillowy
feelings instead of the bitterness rotting my tongue.
It made sense—I longed for the sensuous and sweet
missing from my life.

My father prided himself on his pancakes, one of the few
things he cooked by hand, fluffing the powdery box mix,
taking time to watch the batter bubble on the skillet.
It was one of the few times I saw him still, focused on
something that wasn't in the garage or gaming,
watching cartoons, collecting figures, or
chasing some fresh financial gold mine toward ruin.

Today, homemade pancakes fill the freezer,
my favorite crimson red Tupperware packed to the lid
—blueberry, vanilla, magic masala—perfectly spiced
whole-grains prepared by a peaceful man who
smiles at me across the breakfast table
as I sigh in satisfaction.

I may have wished for unlimited love from my father, but
I more than survived without it. Instead, I've arrived in a
time and space where all my dreams are a mere
moment away from manifesting.

All I have to do is ask.

Tidepool

Ownership: a value of mine—so
let me apologize for my earlier
unaware words.

My wife and I do fight—in the way a
Cancer + Pisces Moon slosh
  feelings
    all over the place

two fish, yin and yang,
   shimmering moonlight fracturing on
water's surface while a
   mother crab
     claws her way to the edge of

  what she believed within the
        bounds of possibility.

We fight for each other.

To Be Contained In His Arms

Life was agonizing for ages—my axis of experience
polarized between excruciating and numb—pleasure,
comfort, safety no more than shimmers, sparks,
magic tricks meant to maintain my hope.

Without warning, I awoke one day to see my soul shining
unadulterated in a mirror—I, a shapeshifting star,
supernova, origin of existence—granted the gift of life.
I remembered the stranger in a black suit never saved me.
Realized no man, flesh or fantasy, ever could. But, if I
released the relationship wreckage with my father,
I'd crack the armor around my heart.

As I forgave myself, Mother, Father, everyone
involved in this story of separation, my love
overflowed, a river carrying me to the cradle of
my lover's arms—the bliss of patience bearing fruit.
Ours is a divine union born of honey-sweet consent,
appreciation, unconditional love, the stability of a
foundation built on friendship, rooted in laughter.

Life Lessons Pt. 2

I taught me:

• Money, all green and glimmer, is important in a society that requires it. I'd rather live in the woods, off the land, with my fingers entwined in lovers' hands.

• Always put yourself first. No sacrifice of self is ever worth it. It does not yield joy; only agony.

• Make promises only if it's to always do your best. Have and respect boundaries. They are the foundation of the world we choose, and there is nothing more powerful than staking that ground.

• Queer identities are fabulous and as individual as every single person that owns a letter of the alphabet. There are as many genders as humans, as many orientations as people who catch our eye.

• My word is not law to anyone but myself. I may take after my mother and my father, but I make myself.

• A woman's body is her own, though other's may attempt to lay claim to it. But, she is also more than a body. She is a mind, a spirit, a feeling. She is everything—the infinite stars in the Universe.

• Never be quiet if you're told to be. That's precisely when it's time to speak up.

• I am whole. Forever, I will exist in the words I have written, in photos, and paintings, in skin cells floating, cosmic dust and dirt. I am saddest when I believe myself forgotten.

But I am not.

Flaws and All

When you were amongst the living, Father,
you were a flawed man like any other.

Your actions, inactions, words and silence,
lack of time, care, or awareness that you had a
daughter desperate to be witnessed,
contributed to some of my keenest wounds,

And I love you.

And I forgive you.

But, now I will no longer be limited by your
lack of energy to give me, no longer will myself to wait,
because now you have no choice.
It was a choice before—all those choices—
when you were amongst the living, Father.

Wherever you are now, at some cosmic bus stop,
I hope you're considering carefully.

What lessons did you learn in this life
so you don't make the same mistakes again?

I hope you will love any
future daughter as if she is
your everything
your strength,
your wisdom,
all your love and
the most valuable
thing in existence.

I could have been that for you,
but I am free now.
Weightless.
Letting go—

I shall be all those things for myself.

And more.

Thank You

To my Father:

Thank you for the laughter that bloomed life when it
sprinkled like June rain. Your Dad jokes hit just right
sometimes, and you never hit me in any other way besides
right in my feelings. Thank you for providing me with
a roof when I needed to get away from one problem,
even if I leapfrogged right into another on your doorstep:
you couldn't have possibly known the trauma chained
to my ankle I was dragging in. Thank you for respecting
my boundaries enough to give me a decade of peace
before bringing me back into the fold of my role as Eldest,
Handler of All Things, Keeper of All Mistakes, First and Last
of Her Line. I know, in this, at last you saw yourself in me—
that finally, too late, you were seeing how capable, strong,
responsible, and kind I had become in spite of everything.
A backhanded compliment, perhaps—putting a stack of
papers in my lap ready to topple, but I will see it for the good
it will one day be and say, *Thank You.*

To my Self:

Thank you for remembering it was okay to laugh, even when
the sky was clouded over, not gray, not blue, but bruised
yellows. Thank you for standing tall in your boundaries,
even when you felt like wilting—a barely-rooted sproutling
clinging to the Earth during a hellish storm. Thank you.
I know it was hard work to fit into shoes you weren't grown
into yet, dragging yourself through calves-deep clay to get
where you needed to go—to your truth, your self, your
authenticity: a magnificent red Maple, all golden and ruby,
sun beaming through outstretched limbs, ready to embrace
the world. Thank you for having the sense to release the
seeds that weren't really yours to plant, ones grafted on by
others, telling you how to be. You are only the roles you
want to play. You are a Jade Moon against a backdrop of
midnight, cut from a cloth emblazoned with millions of
scattered crystals. Luminous. Eldest, But Individual, Keeper
of Poems and Pictures, Handler of a Billion Book Ideas, and
Fueled By Plant Power. Not fat like the insult, but Bigger
Than Life. Not Queer, in the slurred sense, but Queer in
the Unique, One of a Kind, Glorious Rainbow Beauty. Not
an unfaithful cheater, but A Being with Bottomless Love to
Share.

Thank You for letting go of all he told you to be.

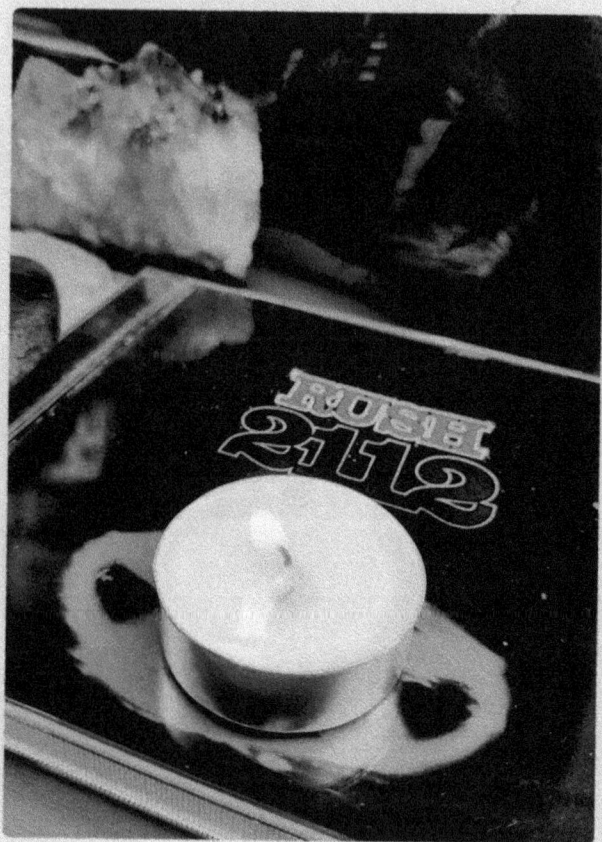

A Ritual to Honor My Heavenly Father

Let Go

Let go of the Anger
Let go of the Pain
Let it fall from your body
Like a fast English rain
Life is not over
But it passes you by
A minute's an hour
in the blink of an eye
While you are dark and sullen
The World still goes on
Don't miss it all looking down,
Look up and move on!

— *A Poem By My Father*

I love you, Dad.

June 27th, 2021

On Writing Daddy's Girl

Q&A with the Author

I'm the kind of reader that really enjoys knowing about the authors whose works I read. I wondered if my audience was the same and as it turns out many of them are. Thank you to the various readers & friends who submitted questions for me to answer!

What was creating *Daddy's Girl* like?

First off, this book was an anomaly. *Daddy's Girl* is the first book I've ever written with a name so clear from the start. Normally, I waffle on names for a while, until suddenly a title clicks into place—or I give up and go with the best mashup of words I sorta like. But as soon as I sat down to scribble the first poem of this volume, the name had already become a solid foundation.

Writing *Daddy's Girl* happened over three stages, spread over a few years: 1) the first drafts between March and August of 2021, 2) revisions and developmental feedback and editing with my poetry editor, Robin Kinzer, in November of 2022, and finally, 3) implementing Robin's feedback and writing 32 new poems in August and September of 2024. This book was over three years in the making because of how much care, attention, and processing needed to go into each piece.

Like my debut poetry book, *A Woman's Work*, I designed *Daddy's Girl* completely by hand—from the cover and interior design to collaborating during every step of the editing process. These poetry collections are like sacred siblings, exploring my out-of-alignment relationship with womanhood and then masculine energy through the lens of my Earthly father. They're complimentary works that share bits and pieces of my story, enough that one could piece together my "lore" in snapshot bits and pieces. Honestly, seeing how they both come together as a matched set is so cool. They're unique glimpses of specific parts of my larger life.

What did you notice as you were writing *Daddy's Girl*? How did this book help you transform?

Earlier this year, 2024, I released *A Woman's Work* which cracked me open rather like an egg right into a frying pan. Holy fuck, I'd done the thing! I shared so much of my story in the most soul-led and authentic way possible. As the cherry on top nod from the Universe, without aiming for it, I landed the #1 new release in both LGBTQ+ Poetry and Contemporary Poetry. What a wild day that was!

I immediately took a sabbatical and integrated all of the

up-leveling that happened as a result of unveiling my voice and truth so powerfully. Because of that experience, I felt fully committed to seeing *Daddy's Girl* through, as painful as I knew it would be.

In my father's dying days in 2021, all of my childhood trauma resurfaced. As I was swept into being the family savior yet again, I was simultaneously experiencing a people-pleaser era so insidious because of how blind I was to it. I was barreling myself toward permanent disability and irreversible chronic illness. Being a *#daddysgirl* was once an important part of my identity, but at this stage, I started to realize it was no longer a badge of honor—it was a mantle of martyrdom.

It was only about two years after my own fibromyalgia diagnosis—and I was in more pain than ever—when I got the call about Dad's worsening diagnosis. He shared his nebulous plans about his estate, revealing my sister and step-mother wouldn't be cared for once he was gone. Before I knew it, dissociated and codependent, I found my way back into the den of depression and despair that was my teenage home.

From there, I began writing poems about my grief and anger—poems like *Clatter of Voices, ScapeGOAT, Grief, In My Defense,* and all the poems surrounding his death and estate. I processed my relationship with my step-mother in poems like *Dear Evil Step-Mother, The Vegan Trinity,*

Step-Monster, and *Obituary*—all written later in 2021 after Dad's passing and the shit show that was his estate. In the end, my step-mother's continued verbal abuse and constant nagging for me to miraculously do what Dad failed to do led me to draw a boundary. I passed his affairs back to the state to be handled because neither of my mother figures volunteered to take over it when I said I was finished.

I took a breather before working with Robin Kinzer on editing the poems I'd already done. Her feedback was wonderful and we had a live workshop session lasting many hours where we refined some of the original poems—the most unrecognizable now being *Roller Coasters & Water Slides* which is so much stronger for it! She also shared the inspiration that eventually led to me doing extensive re-writes in the 2024 writing stint—bringing in more of my flaws and exploring my relationship with other family, too.

Picking the draft back up to edit in 2024 brought this old familiar swell of feelings bobbing right back up to the surface. But, this time, I wasn't in the middle of the swirling chaos. I was standing a few years later—years filled with more healing, unpacking my codependency, couple's therapy, art therapy, growing a business, life coaching, learning my Biological Number, and major spiritual upgrades, each new discovery changing everything all over again.

Now, I saw the wisdom in the poems. I saw the gifts.

As I wrote new content, I found myself creating happier poems—fresh perspectives on myself, my family, and my partnerships. Poems like *In the Spacelab, Papa and the Cows, Sky Fathers, Unlimited Pancakes, The Long Ride Home,* and *To Be Contained In His Arms,* were all tender reflections on how stable I am now.

In 2021, and even the years prior, there was a constant quake of new trauma and triggers because I still couldn't draw boundaries or hold my own against elder's pressures. Today, I am an immovable statue if I truly don't want to do something. It's a night-and-day kind of difference that can only be gained by looking our shame, fear, disappointment, doubt, and dread directly in the eyes, smiling, and choosing to love it all.

How did you turn the trauma you experienced into a triumph through your healing work on yourself?

Authenticity. Self-expression. Healing work (both "shadow" and "light" work). These are a few of the elements that helped me move towards embodiment and my ability to speak and stand in my truth. The journey here was not a quick one, and it took a lot of self-development and hard work.

I've always been a compassionate person, and I am highly sensitive to both energy and emotion, feeling the ripples and waves of the Earth and my fellow beings living here. My purpose is to be in harmony and balance with the world.

I believe strongly in unity and oneness. As a child, I was
the kind of person who would always see the "black sheep"
and ensure they were okay and had a friend in me, at least.
I repaired rifts and mediated conflicts wherever I could.
I quickly learned to caretake others and thus became the
parentified child.

I felt constantly torn between my mother and father. Being
like my mother was not seen as a good thing by anyone
except my mother, and she pushed me to be more like
her than myself. So in many ways, it was easy to cling
to my father as a role model and example of what I was
looking for in a partner, too. He was somewhat hands-off,
but encouraged me to be me in the ways that mom was less
enthusiastic about. He supported me in consuming media
I enjoyed, like anime, and encouraged me to dress in the
goth fashion that I liked. I think I went goth before he did,
but it was a fun period in the "good days" when we twinned
often–wearing similar styles and even matching Hot Topic
looks. During my golden years with my father, mostly when
I was 13 to 15, I was proud to be the child he could connect
with. Then, everything changed.

I represent an unfortunate statistic as a bisexual girl who was
abused in childhood and went on to repeat the cycle in adult
relationships. My youth was rife with pain and trauma, and I
was abused not by just one male parental figure, but by peers
and a friend's brother. While I didn't write a whole poem
about it in this collection, my father not only didn't believe

me about my sexual abuse but also blamed me for "allowing" myself to be sexually assaulted by a peer. I briefly reflect on this in *She's Got Daddy Issues.* My father's denial and hand-waving around my abuse crushed me, perhaps more than anything, for a long time. It was not until I was 30 that I escaped the constant threat of sexual violence. Authenticity was hard to come by when I was constantly in fear and highly codependent.

Throughout those challenging times, I always had tools to self-express: writing fiction and poetry, creating works of art, and exploring myself in other forms in video games and online forums. While those means of sharing my innermost landscapes were wonderful, I still didn't allow myself to speak in full. I held myself back until my mid-30s when I finally began to write my *truth* and share feelings and thoughts openly without fear getting in the way. Writing about my real experiences felt dangerous and impossible, even years after I'd accessed self-love for the first time. It's been a steady unfolding back into self-expression since then.

While I've had extremely low cycles in my life and long patches of rock bottom, I've always come back to believing in myself and my dreams. I felt in my core that things could be better—for me and everyone else, too—even at times when all I knew was suffering. The glimmer in my heart of hope always shone brighter than anything else, drawing me forward like a beacon.

Even when I tried to exit this ride—several attempts to take my own life woven into my adolescent and teen years—my body always knew how to cleanse, purify, and reject the toxins within me, not letting it take its hold for long.

In many ways, I resonate with the Phoenix. I've been told by intuitive friends and professionals that my chart placements and various blueprints are quite that of Phoenix, and that I get to teach other people how to rise in the same way, to use their ashes as the fertile ground from which they are reborn.

It's a metal AF mantle and description, honestly, but as a shadow alchemist and a trauma worker I can't help but see the beauty in the transformation and the magic that comes out of pain.

That's where shadow and light work come in. As my resources and inner capacity grow, so does my tool-kit. I've written a ton about it elsewhere, so I won't go to great lengths here, but I've engaged in many methods of healing over the years—some through exchanges, some through self-learning, and some through access to medical insurance.

I've been blessed to explore: at least twenty therapy modalities; life coaching; spiritual guidance; tarot and oracle readings; Reiki and energy healing; sensory deprivation floating; sauna; dance; journaling; art; fine tuning my nutrition; forest bathing; acupuncture; chiropractic work; breathwork; craniosacral therapy; plant medicine; massage;

EFT tapping; affirmations and manifestation techniques.

My core practice these days includes daily journaling, card pulling, dancing, and using herbal teas and occasional cacao to balance my energy. And, of course, I'm a big fan of cannabis when I use it in a harmonious and supportive way (or to have a blast with friends during game night with lentil crust pizzas).

Overcoming my trauma to this point has taken a lot of self-awareness unpacked through a variety of tools, which requires a willingness to do hard things. I believe in the power of self-expression to heal and liberate, to rise together, and to build better.

P.S. I love this specific question because I once wrote a chapter called "Building the Bridge From Trauma to Triumph: Aligning with Your Soul's Desires," originally published in *The Ultimate Guide to Becoming a Successful Soul Professional*. There, I share about unhooking from a long-term relationship I'd recognized as domestic violence—a relationship where I also experienced financial abuse. As a part of our unhealthy partnership, we opened a healing business with me bankrolling all the initial investments. When the relationship ended, I was left with a mess of paperwork I didn't understand, debt, and a lot of trauma to unpack—not unlike the story of handling my father's estate. In that chapter, I explore how I overcame fear to open my own successful six-figure+ business.

How does your experience impact your work as a healer and how you guide others through their own shadow work?

While I now see and appreciate the transformative beauty in pain, I still know how awful it is to be in the thick of it. I remember what it feels like to be chronically dissociated, chronically ill, in pain and struggling to get by. I've experienced almost every category of trauma except major natural disasters and wars on my doorstep. I get how unfair, senseless, and cruel our suffering feels.

For a long time, I identified as a wounded healer and a victim. Then, I began to identify as a survivor. In both of these cases, I centered my trauma first over my gifts. Even as a trauma therapist, my career and identity were bound up in helping people overcome their trauma.

Now, I see myself as a guide. I've trekked the trails both in shadow and light. I've stumbled a hundred times. I know where the land gets slippery, where the common pitfalls are, and some of the best handholds to grab should you skid on the more challenging terrain.

I walk right alongside you, pointing out some of the areas to watch out for, but also cheering you on, knowing you can do it. I hold with absolute certainty the possibility of overcoming your trauma to where you can feel content in your daily life, neutral about some past experiences, and move in an upward spiral rather than being stuck in a downward spiral. The invitation from the Universe to look at things from a new perspective is always there. I got willing to take a leap of faith and learned to flow through shadow and light alike. Now I can teach others to do the same.

What drives you to put your author identity first at this stage in your life?

Writing has been a lifelong dream for me. I've always wanted to be a "real published author" who could share stories, poetry, and prose to teach lessons in common humanity and decency. There's something magical about the written word—whether it's fiction, poetry, or other forms of prose—that can transcend our modern human squabbles and address overarching issues we need to confront as a species.

The world is rising to face several thorns in our collective side—wounds that cut into our daily experiences, keeping us stuck in an endless cycle of suffering.

To name but a few of these ongoing issues, we have:

— sexism and the suppression of "feminine" energy, impacting people of all genders

— any and all judgements and -isms around people's bodies and identities: whether it be their skin color, level or type of ability, gender, size, spirituality, or anything else

— poverty and lack of access to services, shelter, and food for vulnerable populations

— rampant illness, addiction, and disease

— domestic violence, mass gun crime, war and genocide

— the egregiously high statistics of sexual violence and trafficking

— the destruction of our natural resources, environmental health, and dwindling access to clean food and water sources

All of these things cause trauma and stem from trauma—a ripple passed down from an origin point none of us can even recall. I am here to challenge the normalization of passing on generational trauma. Enough is enough.

I believe in the power of literature to move people and inspire in ways that intellectual discourse sometimes can't. Writing can offer the gift of self-reflection and personal growth, often when people least expect it. My passion lies in creating inclusive narratives across various genres that allow diverse readers to see themselves reflected in words, providing opportunities for them to explore their own hero's journey, or whatever healing path they're on.

The language of storytelling and poetic expression is older than humanity itself, extending into every culture. It's the perfect medium to explore the symbiosis of light and shadow and all the complexities of the human experience. By sharing my poetry, fiction, and other written perspectives, I hope to impact many people, reaching beyond the limitations of one-on-one services.

Ultimately, writing and sharing my work—be it poetry, prose, or fiction—is about healing for myself and others. It's a way to confront and process trauma, integrate difficult experiences, and find meaning in our collective struggles. By putting my vulnerabilities on the page, in whatever form they take, I open up a space for others to do the same. My writing creates a ripple effect of empathy and understanding that can touch countless lives.

Thank you for your part in the journey, dear reader. ♡

References

Pop Culture & Context Notes

This is My Story: "My story" is a reference throughout the book inspired by Final Fantasy X and the character Tidus asking the audience to listen to his story. I consider the narrative of that game by Square Enix to be integral to my own life's story and symbolism.

Life Lessons: Lilith, first wife, refers to the first wife of Adam, who was cast out by a Patriarchal God for being too dominant (she really wanted equity). She was replaced by Eve.

Blank Pages: Final Fantasy X is first directly mentioned in this poem.

The Kindhearted Stranger: Daddy Warbucks is from the play/movie *Annie*. I watched *Annie* a lot as a kid and wouldn't realize until I was much older why I resonated so much with Annie's story and wishes.

print-a-kid: "Bitchin' Camaro" is a song by American rock band the Dead Milkmen. Need For Speed is a video game about car racing. "Widow to the wall" references lyrics from Lil Jon & The East Side Boyz in Get Low (feat. Ying Yang Twins) as featured in Need for Speed. Mini-me and "Did I complete you?" are references to Austin Powers, which was one of my favorite movie series to watch with my father growing up. Hot Wheels are collectible cars. AC/DC, Sex Pistols, Aerosmith, and Rush are all bands.

Grandmas' Girl: *Goosebumps* is a book series by R.L. Stine. Polly Pockets were a line of plastic miniature doll sets. Freaky Friday is the name of a movie, used as an affectionate nickname for me by my Grandmother.

Mini-Dad: Magical girls refers to a genre of anime such as Sailor Moon. More bands are mentioned in this poem: Queen, The Eagles, Sex Pistols, The Clash, Ramones, The Offspring, Blink 182. My Own Worst Enemy is the name of a song by Lit. The final line, "yesterday's child" is a lyric from the song Jaded by Aerosmith (2001). It was one of my favorite songs around that time as I already felt like I was no longer a kid, grown up, and disenfranchised with my existence.

In My Defense: Vana White of Wheel of Fortune Fame–Dad always seemed to like Vana.

subject: Personal letter, nsfw: This is my letter to my father (in entirety), which I sent shortly after he told me he loved my sister more.

Cancer Timelines: Buffle refers to a shorthand version of "Hufflepuff Best Friend," a title shared by a late friend of mine. Our friendship was far shorter-lived than I would have liked.

An Eldest Daughter's Swan Song: The structure and some of the words in stanza 1 are directly inspired and/or borrowed from a madrigal by Orlando Gibbons, "The Silver Swan."

Immune: Starship Enterprise refers to spacecraft in the series, *Star Trek*, originally created by Gene Roddenberry.

In the sweat of thy face shall thou eat bread...: "In the sweat of thy face shalt thou eat bread, till thou return unto the ground; for out of it wast thou taken: for dust thou art, and unto dust shalt thou return." — Genesis 3:19, King James Version (KJV)

Sky Fathers: This poem was written in a ritual while listening to one of my father's favorite albums, 2112 by Rush. This was my first time listening to it, and I have to note I'm still not a fan. Sorry Dad. At any rate, the poem is largely inspired by the open few tracks (often lumped into one track). I borrow the words "my lifeblood spills over" as I found it particularly powerful. The image of space and the red pentagram come from the cover of the album.

Image Notes

In Order of Appearance

Front Cover:
A photo of me at ~14, working with a power tool to grind rust off my dad's old van.

Back Cover:
My 8th grade school picture, in the full swing of being Daddy's Girl.

Daddy's Girl, Then & Now:
Left: A photo of my father and I on a ride at Dutch Wonderland.
Right: A photo of me smoking a joint, hiding in my bathroom in my early 30s.

Cracked Foundations:
Left: A photo of the family home build by Grandma Betty and inherited by my father.
Right: (Top) A photo of me at about 3 years old. (Bottom) Maybe 7 or 8 years old, about to play a game of "Trouble."

Featured alongside the poem *print-a-kid:*
Another photo of me at ~14 working on the rusty van.

A Grief Chapter:
A photo I took of my father during my last visit with him
at the hospital about 3 weeks before he passed on. He is
wearing my color therapy sunglasses, meant to see the world
in a new light.

After Seven Rotations Around the Sun:
The last photograph I took with my father (one of the few
taken in over 12 years). This was just before he went back
into the hospital, on the trip where I tried to help with his
will.

Aftermath:
This photo is of the corkboard in my father's office. The
left-side pinned photo is of my father in high school. On the
right is a school photo of me (grade uncertain, perhaps 7th).
This photo of my father is referenced in the poem *A Jigsaw
(Missing Pieces).*

Rush 2112 Ritual:
A photo recreation of the ritual I did to connect with my
father and heal my relationship with the Divine Masculine.
This is referenced in the poem *Sky Fathers*.

A Note on "Parts"

Internal Family Systems, pioneered as a therapeutic

technique by Richard Schwartz, is likely my favorite therapy and healing approach of the many I've studied. In my poetry work as a whole, I often write about specific Parts of my Self as would be defined by this system. But, Parts is more of a spiritual reality than a psychological invention or technique. Much like in Shamanism, working with Parts of our Self involves being highly resourced, anchored, open, and willing to listen to messages from another world. When we go inside ourselves, we are entering the realms of shadows, of wounds and desires, secrets and fears. It is a vulnerable thing and takes a great deal of care.

Soundtrack

Music is an important tool for emotional processing for me. From dancing it out to finding resonance in lyrics, the power of music to move me is unmatched.

Here are a few songs that really resonated with me while writing and reflecting on this book. Listen, if you wish, for a musical exploration of my emotions through lyrics, vocals, and instrumentals. Each impacted me in some way, all at different stages of my life.

Some of these songs were released recently, and others are from long ago in my past. However, they're ordered by significance to the story arcs represented in the poetry collection.

You're welcome to access my YouTube Music playlist of this soundtrack at *https://tinyurl.com/dgsoundtrack*

CRACKED FOUNDATIONS
Is This It — Jazmin Bean
One Step Closer — Linkin Park
SUN GOES DOWN — Lil Nas X
Inaudible — Manchester Orchestra
Jaded — Aerosmith
Mother's Daughter — Miley Cyrus
VIRUS — GEN.KLOUD

A GRIEF CHAPTER
Mirror — Joshua Bassett
Things That I've Learned — Orla Gartland
Moving Mountains — ANIMA!
LABOUR (the cacophony) — Paris Paloma
Unappreciated — Erica Mason
Way out There — Lord Huron
Don't Fear the Reaper — The Spiritual Machines

AFTERMATH
Burning Pile — Mother Mother
Day By Day — Chris Webby
Lie to Girls — Sabrina Carpenter
It's Alright — Mother Mother
Older — Sasha Alex Sloan
Oldies Station — twenty one pilots

Resources

If you are a trauma survivor and are seeking resources or know someone in need, here are some potential services and sites to access.

Note: Most resources shared are United States specific.

If you are in a crisis situation, please call 911 for physical emergencies and 211 for emotional emergencies.

Text HOME to 741741 to reach a Crisis Counselor via the Crisis Line, or try another hotline such as:

National Suicide Prevention Lifeline
1-800-273-TALK (8255) or Live Online Chat

Domestic Violence Hotline
800.799.SAFE (7233) or visit their website:
https://www.thehotline.org/

The Trevor Project (LGBTQ+)
The Trevor Project specializes in youth LGBTQ+ support.

https://www.thetrevorproject.org/contact-us/

SAMHSA Treatment Referral Helpline
1-877-SAMHSA7 (1-877-726-4727)
Get general information on mental health and locate
treatment services in your area. Speak to a live person,
Monday through Friday from 8 a.m. to 8 p.m. EST.

National Sexual Assault Hotline
Call 800.656.HOPE or chat now at https://rainn.org/

About the Author

Safrianna Lughna, LCPC, MS, aka the Queer-Spirit Guide, is an author, speaker, CEO, and transformational mentor. She began writing poetry when she was eleven years old in order to cope with the traumatic circumstances of her home life. She has notebooks and digital drives full of poems covering everything from heartbreak to healing the planet. Her debut memoir in poetry, *A Woman's Work* is a testament to her personal metamorphosis and her passion for using art to process, express, and ultimately transcend trauma. *Daddy's Girl* is a story about overcoming complex grief and #daddyissues.

Through her writing, Safrianna aims to share transformative words to help brave souls heal from their own harmful experiences and move toward empowered authenticity. After finding healing through artistic expression and spiritual practices, Safrianna evolved beyond her role as a conventional therapist to embrace an intuitive, expansive approach. Today, her work is rooted in mindfulness, the principles of shadow alchemy, holistic wellness, creativity, and ancient traditions.

As an international bestselling author and speaker, her ultimate mission is to inspire others to shine their light and live soul-aligned. Poetry has been a vehicle for healing and transformation for both her and her clients. Through one-on-one guidance, group immersions, creative retreats, and ritual ceremonies, Safrianna compassionately guides others in building bridges from trauma to triumph so they can embrace intentional joy and self-love.

Websites: https://Safrianna.com + https://LivingLUNAs.com
YouTube: https://www.youtube.com/@LivingLUNA
Discord Community: https://discord.me/livingluna
Facebook: https://www.facebook.com/safi.lughna
LinkedIn: https://www.linkedin.com/in/safrianna/

www.ingramcontent.com/pod-product-compliance
Lightning Source LLC
Chambersburg PA
CBHW021504090426
42739CB00007B/456